BARNABE GOOGE

Eclogues, Epitaphs, and Sonnets

BARNABE GOOGE

Eclogues, Epitaphs, and Sonnets

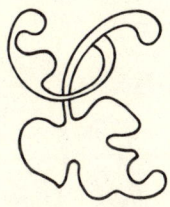

edited by Judith M. Kennedy

UNIVERSITY OF TORONTO PRESS
Toronto Buffalo London

Toronto Buffalo London
Printed in Canada
ISBN 0-8020-2666-4

Printed on acid-free paper

Canadian Cataloguing in Publication Data

Googe, Barnabe, 1540–1594
Eclogues, epitaphs, and sonnets

Includes index.
ISBN 0-8020-2666-4

I. Kennedy, Judith M., 1935– . II. Title.

PR2279.G4A6 1989 822'.3 C89-093145-3

Grateful acknowledgment is made to the Huntington Library, San Marino, California, for permission to reproduce the title-page, coat of arms, and woodcut from Googe's *Eglogs Epytaphes, and Sonettes* (1563) and to Oxford University Press for permission to reproduce fig 52 from Philip Gaskell's *A New Introduction to Bibliography* (1972).

This book has been published with the help of a grant from the Canadian Federation for the Humanities, using funds provided by the Social Sciences and Humanities Research Council of Canada.

Contents

Preface

Barnabe Googe's *Eclogues, Epitaphs, and Sonnets* of 1563 has a recognized place in English literary history as an early instance of English pastoral eclogue, as the first volume in Modern English of lyric poems by a single living author published under his own name, and as a good early exemplar of the plain style of English lyric poetry. However, apart from a 'facsimile' reprint, the whole volume has been edited only once, by Edward Arber in 1871. Because it seems unlikely that the *Eclogues, Epitaphs, and Sonnets* will receive another full-scale edition in the next century or two, this present volume tries to cater to various users. The modernized text, expansive introduction and notes, and brief note on editorial practice are directed primarily to students with little knowledge of the period, offering them a readable text and attempting to arouse their curiosity about other aspects of the period and the ways in which it relates to later Elizabethan literature. At the same time it is hoped that scholars will find that the textual appendix provides the necessary assurances of the reliability of the text, and that they also will find something of interest in the network of literary and personal associations explored in the introduction and notes.

Grateful acknowledgement is made to the Henry E. Huntington Library, the British Library, the Library of Trinity College, Cambridge, the Princeton University Library, and the Harriet Irving Library, Fredericton; to Miss Katharine F. Pantzer; to Mr Robert H. Taylor, and Dr and Mrs B. Juel-Jensen; to Professors William E. Sheidley, Brooke Peirce, Germaine Warkentin, O'Brien Waugh, Beryl Rowland, William A. Ringler, Jr, and James K. McConica; to Mrs Katherine Kennedy; to Miss Prudence Tracy and the University of Toronto Press; to St Thomas University, the Social Sciences and Humanities Research Council, and the Canadian Federation for the Humanities; and to Professor Richard F. Kennedy.

INTRODUCTION

The Life and Times of Barnabe Googe

On 17 November 1558, when Elizabeth succeeded Mary on the English throne, Barnabe Googe was eighteen years old. It was a time of extraordinary excitement, of release and revolution. It was a time of rejoicing, in Holinshed's often quoted words, in the 'lovely sunshine' and 'world of blessings' promised by 'good Queen Elizabeth' after 'the palpable fogs and mist of the most intolerable misery consumed, and the dashing showers of persecution overpast' (4:155). The spirit of renewal and change showed its most obvious effects in politics and religion, but it also breathed energy into the intellectual life of the times. Hope for the future was mixed with uncertainty, but the blend promoted action and involvement rather than hesitation and withdrawal. There were things to do, for writers as well as for statesmen: 'It was not yet time to strike out for a new national literature. Other things were needed first: knowledge of the expanding world, methodological information in all fields, inspiration and guidance for Englishmen and their rulers. For these the writers searched in books imported from the Continent; from sources ancient and modern they produced translations, compilations, and adaptations intended to serve the purpose of the times' (Rosenberg 27).

The centre of this activity was London, 'and London in those days was like Paris in the days of the French Revolution – the heart and brain of a kingdom' (Black 4). Court and Parliament interacted in the process of political and religious revolution, and England's 'third university,' the Inns of Court, swarmed with 'Minerva's men, / And finest wits' who through their literary labours earned 'A princely place in Parnasse hill ... / Where crown of glitt'ring glory hangs, / for them a right reward' (Heywood 102–3). The sense of rebirth in this young reign of the young queen was reflected in the youth of many of these men, 'For who can more Minerva's face / than lusty youth express? / Or where do Muses more delight / than in this youthfulness?' (W.F., in Studley 126). All this intellectual and cultural energy was directed to worthy and moral ends, to enlightening ignorance, and guiding men to do their 'duty in that state of life unto which it shall please God to call' them (*Book of Common Prayer* 286), and to what Sidney calls 'the highest end of the mistress-knowledge, by the Greeks called *architectonike*, which stands (as I think) in the knowledge of a man's self, in the ethic and politic consideration, with the end of well-doing and not of well-knowing only' (*Apology* 104).

Googe was at the centre of this political, religious, and intellectual excitement. By 1559, after his Cambridge years, he was ensconced in Staple Inn. He was a kinsman (and later ward) of the most influential man in the kingdom, the Queen's Secretary, Sir William Cecil. He was encouraged in his literary endeavours by the learned and the famous, and it was even before the publication of the first part of his translation of Palingenius's *Zodiacus vitae* (*Zodiac of Life*) that he was named among the Minerva's men and finest wits. He saw the religious 'revolution' by which the church of his faith was established (Dickens 401). He witnessed in France and Spain the effects of England's new political directions. And he fell in love.

The poems in this volume are the response of a young man to the challenges of the first years of Elizabeth's reign, as well as to those of his own intellectual and emotional explorations. More broadly, his life and works illustrate many aspects of the age.[1]

FAMILY AND FRIENDS IN KENT

Googe was born in 1540, probably on 11 June, St Barnabas Day. His father was Robert Goche (variously spelt Gooch, Gogher, or Googe) of Lincolnshire, his mother Margaret Mantell, daughter of Sir Walter Mantell of Heyford, Northamptonshire. His parents were married at Bekesborne in Kent on 18 June 1539; his mother died on 24 July 1540. His father remarried in 1552, and died in 1557, when Barnabe became an unsold ward of the Court.

Googe probably received the grammar school education that was becoming normal for the sons of the gentry, and it seems had a schoolmaster who provided a standard of awesomeness in later life: from Ireland in 1583 he wrote, 'I was never more afraid of my schoolmaster than I am of [dysentery], and yet I trust in God to escape it' (Pinkerton 241). In 1555 he matriculated pensioner at Christ's College, Cambridge, and by 1559 had entered Staple Inn in London. The influences of this standard educational pattern can be seen in the topics and style of his writings.

The major personal influences on Googe's career stem from family relationships, particularly the nexus of kindred and friends connected with his maternal grandmother, and the association with Sir William Cecil. Perhaps because of a sometimes violently expressed antipathy for his stepmother, which ended only with her death in 1584, it appears that Googe spent considerable time in Kent with 'the right worshipful and his especial good Grandmother my Lady Hales,' as he calls her in dedicating to her in March 1560 the first three books of his translation of Palingenius.[2] His grandmother had taken as her third husband Sir James Hales, whose house 'the Dungeon' near Canterbury provided Googe the opportunity for some punning in 'To Mistress D.' (30). The influence of his grandmother, of his step-grandfather, and of his Kentish relations, friends, and acquaintances is strongly apparent in Googe's early writing. Paying tribute to Lady Hales after her death, Googe emphasizes 'her special love and delight in God, and in his service,' her devoted aid to the poor and those afflicted with 'loathsome' diseases, 'her mild and sweet disposition, her great humility, and carelessness of the vain world' (Heresbach 167v). Both her godliness and her humility seem reflected not only in Googe's choice for translation of the work of the 'most Christian' and 'godly and zealous' Palingenius, whose poem discloses 'the heinous crimes and wicked vices of our corrupt nature' and declares 'the pleasant and perfect pathway into eternal life,' but also in his doubts about his ability to undertake the translation, and in his trust that by attempting it he will 'do no less profit to my country than service to God.'[3]

Despite Googe's emphasis on his grandmother's good works, this side of his family was as firmly Protestant (in Anglican terms) as the Cecil connection. In his third eclogue Googe could have had in mind many 'seely sheep' and 'good shepherds' who were consumed with flames, vexed, tormented, and driven out by the hateful hounds of hell during the Marian persecution, but none closer to home than his step-grandfather. Sir James Hales was an eminent lawyer and judge, and, like the William Lovelace to whom Googe dedicates the *Eclogues, Epitaphs, and Sonnets*, reader of Gray's Inn (in 1533, 1537, and 1540) and sergeant-at-law (in 1540). He was created a knight of the Bath at Edward VI's coronation in 1547. Among his many duties in Edward's reign was participation in the commissions that deprived Bishops Bonner and Gardiner. Although shortly after her accession Mary renewed his patent of justice of the common pleas, Gardiner (now Lord Chancellor) soon had his revenge. Hales was imprisoned, where under the pressure of theological dispute 'he attempted to commit suicide by opening his veins with his penknife.' Released in April 1554, he 'went mad and drowned himself in a shallow stream' near his Kentish home (*DNB* 8:913; see also Eccles 354). It is not surprising that Googe's first appearance in print should have been in a poem prefixed to *A Brief Treatise ... of the Pope's Usurped Primacy*,[4] in which he exhorts the men of Romish sect to forsake the wicked ways of the 'haughty whore' of Rome (see pp 125–6). The work is dedicated to an eminent Marian exile, the Protestant divine Thomas Becon, who by 1559 had been restored to his place as one of the 'six preachers' at Canterbury (*DNB*).

Another famous combatant for the Protestant cause, John Bale, had also returned to England in 1559, and on 10 February 1560 was admitted to a canonry at Canterbury Cathedral (Fairfield 144). Whether Googe met him in London or in Canterbury, by December 1559 Bale was encouraging Googe to persist with the translation of Palingenius (Dedicatory epistle, Palingenius 1560). Googe's gratitude to and affection for him find expression in the attractive poem 'To Doctor Bale' (18). Yet another eminent returning exile, Alexander Nowell, had connections both with Cecil and with Kent: Cecil had included his name in a list of divines to receive preferment, and in February 1560 he was given the rectory of Saltwood with Hythe in Kent, and a canonry at Canterbury Cathedral (*DNB* 14:689). Googe's poem 'To Master Alexander Nowell' (17) is sometimes awkwardly phrased, but the warmth of his admiration is conveyed in the emphasis on the joy inspired by Nowell's steadfastness in sacred learning.

Kentish relatives and friends are also important at this stage of Googe's development. Not only learned Master Bale, but also cousin Honywood and uncle Mantell urged him on in translating Palingenius. Googe's Latin epistle in the 1560 edition is directed to Thomas Honywood, William Cromer, and 'Ra. Heimundo' (?Ralph Hayman), all of whose names appear in Lambarde's 1576 list of the names of the nobility and gentry of Kent, together with that of Sir Henry Cobham (see 'To M. Henry Cobham of the most blessed state of Life' [23]).[5] William Lovelace, sergeant-at-law, the dedicatee of the *Eclogues, Epitaphs, and Sonnets*, is a name added by Lambarde himself to the list of nobility and gentry (originally compiled by the heralds during the visitation of Kent in 1574), as are the names of Barnabe 'Gooche,' Alexander and Thomas Neville, and Thomas and George Darrell (and 'Sir Henry Sidney, Knight of the Garter, Lord Deputy of Ireland, and Lord President of Wales').

Alexander Neville and his younger brother Thomas were Googe's cousins (their mother Anne being the sister of Googe's mother Margaret), and are important partly in literary associations with

Googe, and partly for the connections they provide with other literary figures. Alexander was four years younger than Barnabe, but the several poetic exchanges in this volume show a friendship based on common interests as well as blood ties. Alexander was a precocious student: his translation of Seneca's *Oedipus* was printed by Colwell in April of 1563, but according to a sentence that Alexander added to the dedication when the play was reprinted in Newton's collected *Seneca his Tenne Tragedies* of 1581, he actually made the translation in his sixteenth year (187). In other words (if his rather dissembled parade of youthfulness is to be believed (see Spearing 359–63)), he was engaged on the translation of Seneca when Googe was similarly engaged with Palingenius. Like Googe, Alexander was educated at Cambridge and the Inns of Court. A connection with Cecil may be seen in his dedication of *Oedipus* to his godfather, Nicholas Wotton, a 'specialist civil servant' and 'veteran diplomat' who was a member with Cecil of the Queen's privy council, and accompanied him in 1560 on the 'spectacularly successful' mission that resulted in the treaty of Edinburgh (MacCaffrey 32, 82, 85). Wotton and Cecil's association was longstanding and friendly: when Wotton was in Paris in 1553 he wrote offering to buy books for Cecil there (McKisack 50). While Alexander was in London he exercised his poetic talents in exchanges with George Gascoigne as well as with his cousin Barnabe. But his main interests were more scholarly. At the age of nineteen he already found Seneca's plays rather light, and was expecting 'to bestow my travail in matters of far greater weight and substance' (Dedication to *Oedipus*). His studiousness found scope in his post as secretary to Archbishop Parker, in whose house, 'a kind of flourishing University of learned men,' with others who 'truly and sincerely feared God,' he was able 'to pursue learning and piety with an ardent desire.'[6] The cousins shared the experiences of Cambridge, Canterbury, and London, and responded to the stimulus with similar efforts to pass on their learning and sense of moral purpose. The differences between them are also instructive. Neville's Epistle and Preface to *Oedipus* are more sententious and self-confident in tone than Googe's supporting prose and poetry to the 1560 Palingenius translation; he verges on the priggish, and quite lacks Googe's self-deprecatory humour. Their responses to Kett's rebellion are also diverse: Googe writes an English poem imbued with personal indignation ('The Epitaph of the Lord Sheffield's death' [13]), while his cousin publishes twelve years later a scholarly Latin history (see pp 224–6).

Neville's later career does not illuminate the background of the poems in this volume, but does give clues to possible later readers, particularly in the circles of Sidney and Spenser. Thomas Drant, now chiefly remembered for his rules for quantitative versification, was Alexander's contemporary at Cambridge and in the 1560s was engaged in imitations and translations of the classics, some of them addressed to Cecil and his wife.[7] He contributed a long Latin dedicatory poem to Neville's account of Kett's rebellion, addressed to 'his friend, naturally endowed with and thoroughly polished in all attributes of a liberal education' ('Alex. Ne. amico suo ingenuo atque omni humanitate perpolito'). In 1587 Neville compiled and contributed to a collection of Latin, Greek, and Hebrew poems, the lament of Cambridge University upon the death of Sidney. M.W. Wallace calls him 'an esteemed friend of Philip' (106), and his poem was praised by the Queen's godson, Sir John Harington.[8] Neville spent his life in Canterbury, after Archbishop Parker's death serving his successors Grindal and Whitgift until his own death in 1614.[9]

COURTSHIP AND MARRIAGE

The other Kentish family of particular importance to Googe at the time he was writing the poems of this volume was that of the Darrells. The daughter of Thomas Darrell, Mary, was to be the busy and faithful wife of Googe's lifetime, but not until after a courtship that had its tempests. She is most likely the Mistress D. of the poem so addressed (30), in which Googe laments that her 'faithful servant ... so long doth lack / his own dear mistress' sight.' Perhaps, too, it was her name that he amusingly condemns his 'cursed hand' for not drawing in 'Of the unfortunate choice of his Valentine' (38). The problems of the courtship did not surface until the summer of 1563 (after the publication of these poems). The surviving correspondence does most justice to the passions involved, but even a summary of events may convey something of the emotional drama (see Googe *Eglogs* [1871] 9–14). Briefly, Mary's father wanted to marry her to a wealthier suitor, Sampson Lennard, son of John Lennard of Chevening in Kent. Despite Cecil's direct intervention on Googe's behalf, both John Lennard and Thomas Darrell denied that there had been any previous agreement or bond between Barnabe and Mary, and Lennard complained to Cecil of Googe's 'hot head' and 'sick brain,' and his threats to Darrell that 'he would tell the Queen of him.' The threats were not one-sided. In a 'scornful letter' to Mary's cousins George and Edward Darrell, Googe writes of 'the martial furniture that hath been prepared against me, and the Italian inventions that have been menaced against me.' Under pressure from her parents, 'to whom I am both by the law of God and nature bound to give honour and obedience,' Mary wrote to Googe, 'I heartily beseech you, gentle Master Googe, if ever any true love or goodwill you have borne towards me, cease and leave off from all further suit or means to me in this matter.' The letter is signed 'From my father's house at Scotney this Thursday the xxth of October.' But Lennard's wealth was not a match for Googe's powerful connections. Cecil had enlisted the aid of Archbishop Parker who, after questioning Mary and finding her 'firm and stable to stand to that contract she had made,' sequestered her out of her parents' hands into 'the custody of one Mr Tufton a right honest gentleman.' Parker informed Cecil that he intended 'to go *plane et summarie* to work, to spare expenses, which Mr Lennard and the wilful parents would fain incur to weary the young Gentleman, paraventure not superfluously moneyed so to sail the seas with them.' They were married on 5 February 1564, and it appears that bad feelings were soon overcome. The young couple settled at Lamberhurst on the border of Sussex and Kent, the same parish in which Mary's home Scotney lay, and not long after Googe sold land to her brother and dedicated a book to her sisters.[10] Googe's passion and determination in his own love affair give strength to his poetic explorations of the sometimes destructive power of misdirected or thwarted love.

LONDON AND THE INNS OF COURT

Although Googe's first publications in March 1560 show his strong ties with Kent, he was already resident at Staple Inn, and beginning to taste the pleasures offered by the Inns of Court. Their attractions have been well described by W.R. Prest: 'Their geographical location made them ideally suited to introduce young men to the exciting world of London, already the mecca of ambition and talent, the kingdom's administrative, commercial, cultural and political hub. The inns provided convenient communal accommodation midway between City and Court. For most young gentlemen who wished to spend some time in London, an inn of court was the logical place to stay ... "where it is probable they will find their friends, and can never miss men of good manners and good conversation"' (21). Prest's quotation from the Earl of Clarendon is apt, but the early Elizabethan inns offered more than good manners and good conversation. They were at the very heart of the intellectual and cultural ferment of the day. Plays at the Inns of Court, beginning with *Gorboduc*, performed at the Inner Temple at the Christmas revels of 1561–2, contributed significantly to the development of vernacular drama. The association with Court and university was close. *Gorbuduc* was performed before the Queen at Court on 18 January 1562; Richard Edwards, Master of the Children of the Chapel Royal from 1561, was elected to Lincoln's Inn in 1564, and staged his plays at Oxford as well as in London (Wilson 132–3, 111–12; Conley 25–6). That Googe was excited by the new drama is evident from the lively impudent tone of his question to Plautus and Terence in 'Of Edwards of the Chapel': 'What would you say, sirs, if you should behold, / As I have done, the doings of this man?' (20.13–14) – the answer is burst into tears and burn their books! 'Good conversation' also included poetic exchanges, such as those of Googe with Neville and with Blundeston, who was a member of Gray's Inn (F.B. Williams 19). Young men wishing 'to abandon all vain delights' for the study of law might be forced so to prove their poetic abilities: Alexander Neville with four other 'sundry gentlemen' of Gray's Inn in 1565 required George Gascoigne 'to write in verse somewhat worthy to be remembered, before he entered into their fellowship' (Gascoigne 62). Once received into that fellowship poets could expect support and encouragement. Googe obviously expected from William Lovelace, sergeant-at-law and reader of Gray's Inn, 'the friendly receiving' of the poems of this volume, and Gascoigne also found Sergeant Lovelace 'many ways my friend' (181). But the most pervasive intellectual activity was translation, especially of the classics both ancient and more recent. C.H. Conley provides a number of facts to substantiate the claim that 'though the liberal and popular renaissance movement originated at Cambridge in the reigns of Henry and Edward, the majority of its supporters in the reign of Elizabeth were to be found at the inns of court working together for the spread of new ideas' (27).

KINSMAN TO CECIL

One of the most important of those supporters was Sir William Cecil. He had been part of the earlier movement during his years at Cambridge in 1535–41, and after leaving Cambridge had studied at Gray's Inn. The links forged at university were maintained at Court. As B.W. Beckingsdale points out: 'John Cheke taught Edward VI. Roger Ascham and William Grindal taught the Princess Elizabeth. Thomas Smith became Secretary of State. The result was that those who had been readers, professors and fellows, lecturers and students at Cambridge when Cecil was an undergraduate, were to be found at Court when Cecil entered public life' (17). Cecil married Cheke's sister Mary (despite his parents' opposition), but she died less than a year after the birth of their son Thomas in 1542. In 1545 Cecil married Mildred, eldest of the famously learned daughters of Sir Anthony Cooke, Governor of Prince Edward, thus strengthening his ties with the Protestant movement of religious and educational reform. During his virtual retirement in Queen Mary's reign, Cecil continued to serve as Surveyor to Princess Elizabeth, and upon her accession was rapidly established as one of her most trusted advisers. One of the rewards for his service was appointment as Master of the Court of Wards, to which lucrative office he succeeded on 10 January 1561 (Beckingsale 89).

At this date Googe was still himself a ward of the court, as well as being connected to Cecil by kinship and by the services his father Robert had performed for Cecil in earlier years (Barnett 66). It seems that his personal relationship with Cecil had strengthened during 1560, and the second instalment of the translation of Palingenius is dedicated not to his grandmother, but 'To the right honourable and his singular good Master, Sir William Cecil, Knight. One of the most honourable Privy Council, Master of the Wards, and Liveries, and Secretary to the Queen's highness.' Since the dedication is dated 'the iii. Ides of January' (presumably 11 January), Googe lost no time in acknowledging Cecil's new honour. The epistle itself so well expresses the aims of the translation movement and Googe's attitude to poetry that it is reprinted in full in the present volume (pp 132–4). The epistle also shows Googe's continuing reading: Justin, Plato, and Lucretius are added to the classical authors mentioned in 1560. 'Justin' refers to the abridgment of the histories of Trogus Pompeius made by Justinus, a work that so took Googe's fancy that he expanded the Table of 'Poetical words' to include the anecdotes of Bubalus and Tirtaeus mentioned in the epistle. Trogus may have been brought to his attention by Thomas Norton, student of the Inner Temple, co-author of *Gorboduc*, and like Googe one of the Minerva's men praised by Heywood, who in 1560 published a volume of politically oriented *Orations*, one drawn from Trogus; or by Arthur Golding, whose translation of the whole was entered in the Stationers' Register in 1562–3 and published in 1564; or by Roger Ascham who laments that the habit of epitome has meant the loss of Trogus' original work (106). All three men share an association with Cecil, whose extraordinary political accomplishments have overshadowed his importance as a patron of learning and the arts.

It is not possible here to explore all the implications for Googe's intellectual development of his access to Cecil's home and circle, but perhaps two retrospective accounts may give some impression of that society. The first, a famous one, is Ascham's description in *The Schoolmaster* of the dinner party in Cecil's chamber at Windsor Castle that prompted Sir Richard Sackville (father of the co-author of *Gorboduc*) to ask Ascham to write his treatise of education, 'seeing God did so bless you to make you the scholar of the best master [Sir John Cheke], and also the schoolmaster of the best scholar [Queen Elizabeth], that ever were in our time' (9).[11] In Book II, musing on the ways that learning is fostered, Ascham sees Cecil as a towering influence since that momentous day, 17 November 1558. Particularly in his capacity as Chancellor of Cambridge University, Cecil 'hath the present oversight of the whole chase, who was himself sometime, in the fairest spring that ever was there of learning, one of the forwardest young plants in all that worthy College of St John's, who now by grace is grown to such greatness as, next the providence of God and goodness of one, in these our days *religio* for sincerity, *literae* for order and advancement, *respublica* for happy and quiet government have, to great rejoicing of all good men, specially reposed themselves.' That Googe is part of this reposing or re-establishing of letters in the protection of Cecil's greatness is recognized by Ascham: 'Indeed Chaucer, Thomas Norton of Bristol, my Lord of Surrey, Master Wyatt, Thomas Phaer, and other gentlemen in translating Ovid, Palingenius, and Seneca have gone as far, to their great praise, as the copy they followed could carry them' (although he wishes they could have been 'more like unto the Grecians than unto the Gothians in handling of their verse') (137, 145–6). The implied coupling of Golding and Googe is frequent in references in the sixteenth century, and emphasizes the influence of Cecil. Golding, as uncle and tutor of Cecil's ward the young Earl of Oxford,[12] was resident in Cecil House, which through its master's personal care for those in his guardianship became so famed as an academic establishment that 'there was competition to secure a place in it for wards and sons. Lady Stanhope, the Countess of Lennox, Lady Russell, the Earl of Essex, the Duke of Norfolk, the Bishop of Ely and Sir Henry Sidney were among those who sought to put children in Burghley's care' (Beckingsale 248).

The second retrospective account illustrating that milieu comes from one of those wards, Arthur Hall, who in 1581 dedicated his translation of *Ten Books of Homer's Iliads* to Cecil's elder son Thomas. In his dedication he recalls the time that he translated the first fragments, when he 'groped thereat, being a Scholar with you in my Lord your father's house.' Taking them up again, he completes the translation (from French, not Greek), but wonders whether to publish the results:

> when I considered of the ripe wits of this age, and had read diverse works so exquisitely done in this kind by our own Nation, as the travail of M. Barnabe Googe in Palingenius, the learned and painful translation of part of Seneca by M. Jasper Heywood, the excellent and laudable labour of M. Arthur Golding, making Ovid speak English in no worse terms than the author's own gifts gave him grace to write in Latin, the worthy works of that noble Gentleman my L. of Buckhurst [Thomas Sackville], the pretty and pithy conceits of M. George Gascoigne, and others in great numbers ... when I minded, I wished I had been otherwise occupied, I condemned my travails, I scratched my head as men do, when they are greatly barred of their wills.

He is most daunted by thoughts of Phaer's Virgil, which Googe praises so highly in 'An Epitaph of Master Thomas Phaer' (15), but he remembers the encouragement he had received 'about 18 or 19 years past' from Ascham and Heywood, and decides to proceed. Hall's references to his 'ungoverned youth' and to the 'contraries' that made him insufficiently responsive to the 'honourable and rare favour' of Cecil, indicate that he shared the tastes of his friend, the troublesome Thomas, and according to the account in the DNB his life was indeed extremely wild, but even in this erratic personality the seeds of Cecil's training bore some fruit.

TRAVEL ABROAD

One way in which Cecil tried to further the education of his elder son was by foreign travel, sending him to Paris in 1561. In Thomas's case the effort was productive only of more trouble (Read 212–17), but Googe's excursion to the continent in the same year at least blossomed in poetry, in the three travel poems (43, 44, 45), and in the translations and imitations from the current Spanish bestseller *Diana* of Montemayor (9, 11, 47). Googe travelled through France to Spain and Portugal in the train of Sir Thomas Chaloner, Cecil's close friend who had just been appointed ambassador to Spain. Chaloner was a scholar and a poet as well as a diplomat. He had published a translation of Erasmus's *Praise of Folly* in 1549, and in 1560 dedicated to Queen Elizabeth a Latin panegyric on Henry VIII. His lengthy Latin poem *De republica Anglorum instauranda decem libri*, the first five books of which were dedicated to

Cecil, was largely written during his Spanish appointment. When the work appeared in 1579, fourteen years after his death, it had appended to it a number of shorter Latin poems, including ones on Shelley and Phaer, which Peirce believes Googe may have seen (323; see also DNB 3:1366–7, McConica 258, and Eccles 358–9). Among the members of Chaloner's train was Googe's Kentish friend Henry Cobham (see 23). No wonder that in such stimulating company Googe began to acquaint himself with contemporary masterworks of Spanish literature such as Garcilaso's *Eclogues* and Montemayor's *Diana*.

Googe returned to England in the summer of 1562, probably on a ship leaving Bilbao on 1 June, and found that the poems he had left with his friend Laurence Blundeston were in the hands of the printer. Since publication of an anthology of one's own verses was in 1563 without precedent in modern English, Googe's reaction to this discovery appears understandably reluctant. How far he may have been party to the scheme, and the modifications he made to the collection after his return, are discussed on p 19 and in the Textual Appendix.

LATER YEARS

After his marriage in February 1564, Googe divided his time among his family, his service to Cecil (created Lord Burghley in 1571), and his writing. His first accomplishment was to complete the translation of Palingenius, which was published on 18 April 1565, although in his dedicatory epistle to Cecil Googe understandably complains that he had not enjoyed 'so quiet a mind as had been needful for such a labour.' Three or four years later he wrote a book called 'The Counterfeit Christian,' intended for his sisters-in-law; when it 'by ill-favoured fortune perished,' he hastily wrote instead a poem called 'The Ship of Safeguard,' 'because of the dangers of this world, whereby the soul enclosed in the bark of the sinful flesh with great hazard passeth.' Together with two verse 'stories' drawn from Rufinus's version of Eusebius's *Ecclesiastical History*, this poem was published in February 1569, and dedicated to 'his very good sisters.' A more ambitious and more directly political work of this period was his translation of Thomas Kirchmeyer's 'The Popish Kingdom,' published together with two books of the same author's 'Spiritual Husbandry' in 1570. This volume was dedicated to the Queen herself. Possibly John Bale originally drew the work to Googe's attention, but his decision to translate and publish it at this time may have been prompted by the

Catholic-inspired Northern Rebellion of 1569, which he seems to glance at in his comment in the dedicatory epistle on 'the feigned sanctity of the Romish religion that now so much is boasted of.' Perhaps the Queen thanked him for his efforts when he was 'first server for the first meal' during her visit to Burghley at Theobalds in 1572 (Barnett 66).

The next recorded service that Googe performed for Burghley was to visit Ireland in the first half of 1574, to report on Essex's expedition. He was very sick with dysentery, but still spent his time to such good purpose that he earned Essex's 'friendly report' and 'recommendation' that Burghley would 'encourage him in this good desert' (Pinkerton 184). Upon his return to England Googe revised Palingenius for a new edition in 1576, again dedicated to his great kinsman Burghley, and published two more translations in 1577, *The Overthrow of the gout* by Christopher Balista and *Four Books of Husbandry* by Conrad Heresbach. Both of these may show Burghley's influence, since he suffered from gout, and was notably interested in husbandry and horticulture. The Heresbach is dedicated to Sir William Fitzwilliam (brother-in-law of Sir Henry Sidney), who was Lord Deputy of Ireland when Googe was there in 1574. His service in Ireland had been long and difficult, and the retirement granted to him in 1575 eagerly sought (*DNB* 7:232–5). The terms in which his 'assured loving friend' Googe dedicates this bucolic work to him are entirely consistent with the spirit of his youthful eclogues and moral poems: for the good service of his youth it is right that Fitzwilliam should have 'rest and quietness,' and 'there is, in my fancy, no life so quiet, so acceptable to God, and pleasant to an honest mind, as is the life of the Country, where a man, withdrawing himself from the miserable miseries, vanities, and vexations of this foolish and now too too much doting world, may give himself to the sweet contemplation of God, and his works, and the profit and relief of his poor distressed neighbour, to which two things we were chiefly created.' Googe adds to the original text anecdotes and information from his own reading and experience, creating a delightful and practical work that deserved its frequent reprintings.

Irish associations also prompted his next publication, a prose address 'To my very loving friend Captain Barnabe Rich' prefatory to Riche's pamphlet of 1578, *An Alarm to England*.

Apart from the translation of a curious pamphlet on a 'miracle drug' published in 1587, Googe's last literary work was the translation of the *Proverbs* of Lopez de Mendoza, Marquis of Santillana, dedicated to Burghley by 'Your Lordship's faithful servant Barnabe Googe.' The work appealed to Googe because it seeks to train readers 'to honesty and virtuous life' and because 'there is nothing assuredly more acceptable to God, nor that indeed better beseemeth man, than an upright and honest conversation.'

In 1582 Googe, apparently in financial difficulties, returned to Ireland as Provost Marshall of the Presidency Court of Connaught, from whence he corresponded with Walsingham and Burghley, still relying on Burghley's help for his large and hopeful family: 'My poor wife I have left in England, who beside the charge of divers of my children that she keepeth at grammar school and abroad, is greatly charged with a couple of them at the University. I beseech your Lordship, if she have any reasonable suit to your Lordship, that it would please your Lordship to be favourable to her' (From Athlone, 11 March 1583; in Pinkerton 241). In September 1583 he returned to England, but by October 1584 he was again in Ireland, now anxious to dispose profitably of his office so that he could retire to England to take possession of the lands now finally available to him after the death of his stepmother. This he achieved by April of 1584. He spent the remainder of his life at Alvingham, where he died in February 1594.

The Literary Context of the *Eclogues, Epitaphs, and Sonnets*

The small volume of poems that Googe published in 1563 has attracted the attention of literary historians and critics for several reasons: it is the first collection of short personal poems published by a single author in his own lifetime in Modern English; the eclogues it contains provide one of only two earlier English analogues to Spenser's *Shepheardes Calender*; and the plain style of his lyrics has made them important to those critics who see the mainstream of English poetic achievement in the Elizabethan age represented in such writers as Gascoigne, Greville, Raleigh, and Donne rather than Sidney, Spenser, Daniel, and Drayton.

Although at the time of publication Googe's friends made high claims on his behalf, they do not particularly emphasize the unusual nature of the enterprise. It is instructive to compare Neville's and Blundeston's prefatory verses and epistles with the epistle to Harvey prefacing Spenser's *Shepheardes Calender*, signed by the still-unidentified E.K. In both cases the example and authority of Chaucer are invoked, in both the poet is praised for his skill, and advised to ignore critics (all predictable topics paralleled in other prefaces of the Elizabethan age). But there are two striking differences in substance, apart from the general contrast provided by E.K.'s greater sophistication and parade of learning: E.K. is introducing a poet 'uncouthe unkiste,' whereas Googe is already known for his 'famous writings'; E.K. repeatedly emphasizes that he is introducing 'the *new* Poete,' and in everything that he praises the new Poet for, he stresses the novelty of his achievement, and the barrenness of what has gone before. Neville encourages Googe to pursue his 'famous deeds' to win 'present praise' and 'immortal fame,' but neither he nor Googe shows any consciousness of breaking new ground towards the establishment of an English literature that might rival the greatest works of other nations past and present. Googe's eclogues are not perceived as the first trial of his tender wings before he makes the greater flight of epic composition. Nevertheless the first step towards assertion of the highest personal poetic ambition can perhaps be seen in Blundeston's prose address, when he presents the volume as 'this pattern for others to follow,' (*3.39–40). Others did follow, of course, in the next fifteen or sixteen years – Turbervile, Howell, Gascoigne, Breton, Churchyard – some perhaps best forgotten, some undeservedly neglected, all rather ungenerously treated by most of the younger generation of Sidney, Spenser, and their circles. The literary climate during the early part of Elizabeth's reign was different. Then, even translation of epic poetry was seen as a commendable activity in itself, and writers were more eager to claim that England already had the resources to match the achievements of other ages and other countries, as Googe himself said in 1560, 'So much doth England flourish now / With men of Muses' kind' (p 131). It may be said that it was because so much had already been done by 1579 that Sidney and Spenser were able to see their way to higher peaks.

The conscious effort in the mid-century to store the English language, which had been chiefly concentrated on translation, was seen not only as providing instruction for the unlearned, particularly those lacking Latin, but also as training native writers. As Phaer writes in the endnote following Book VII of his 1558 translation of the *Aeneid*, he would be happy if someone else completed the task, 'contenting myself sufficiently with this, that by me first, this gate is set open. If now the young writers will vouchsafe to enter, they may find in this language, both large and abundant camps of variety, wherein they may gather innumerable sorts of most beautiful flowers, figures, and phrases, not only to supply the imperfection of me, but also to garnish all kinds of their own verses with a more clean and compendious order of metre, than heretofore commonly hath been accustomed' (x2v).

Googe's much-praised contribution to the early years of this central effort was his translation of Palingenius's *Zodiacus vitae*. The Italian author of this immensely popular, encyclopedic philosophical poem was considered an important voice of the Reformation, not least because 'his bones were exhumed and burnt, and his book placed upon the Index in 1558, among writings of heretics of the first class' (Tuve, in Palingenius vi). In the first poems of his collection of original verse, the eclogues, Googe is deeply indebted to another Italian, Mantuan, whose *Bucolica*, like the *Zodiacus* was a popular school text. Although a Carmelite, Mantuan too was seen as a light of the Reformation because of his strong criticism of clerical abuses. Together with such ancient authors as Ovid and Seneca, these modern continental writers helped to stock and polish Googe's poetry. When the occasion arose of publishing his own poems, he appears also to have looked to continental models for the organization and presentation of the volume.

The story told in the prefatory material of the *Eclogues* of the overzealous friend who unbeknownst to the author sent his works to the printer and forced him reluctantly to consent to publication can be seen as an example of the elaborate subterfuges that were resorted to in order to allow a gentleman poet to appear in print, but there are bibliographical indications that the story is true, and that Googe was not a willing partner in the initiative. Once committed to the enterprise, however, it appears that he took considerable pains to revise, add to, and arrange his poems. He himself acknowledges preparing 'Cupido Conquered,' when he apologizes for 'my too hastily finished Dream, the greater part whereof with little advice I lately ended' (2.40–2), and the physical evidence of the volume indicates that the printer had to accommodate revisions to the Eclogues (see the Textual Appendix).

What models were available to Googe when he attempted to give some polish to the 'paper bunch' of his youthful and familiar verses so precipitately committed to the printer's hands? Closest to him was of course *Songes and Sonettes, written by the ryght honorable Lorde Henry Haward late Earle of Surrey, and other*, now most commonly known as Tottel's *Miscellany*, in which Grimald's poems provide some precedent for the publication of assorted verse by an identified living author. Continental collections of Neo-Latin verse, such as the often reprinted *Carmina quinque illustrium poetarum*, featuring such august early sixteenth-century writers as Bembo and Castiglione, also gave a precedent of social respectability, but such compilations, although presenting varied types of verse, do not reveal the self-conscious divisions of Googe's *Eclogues, Epitaphs, and Sonnets*, with the annexed 'Dream.' The closest parallels to Googe's volume are provided by Clément Marot's *L'Adolescence Clémentine* and the *Poemata* of Théodore de Bèze, or Beza. Both are volumes of mainly original short poems published by one living author; both consist of youthful poems and are presented with protestations of reluctance; both consciously divide the poems into types. Moreover, both authors were prominent in the movement of religious reform, and translations from both appear in Tottel's *Miscellany*.

Marot's volume was first published in 1532, when he was thirty-six years old and already famous. In a preface 'to a great number of his brothers, all children of Apollo,' he discusses his reasons for publishing the poems (pressure from friends, and pirated versions), and emphasizes the youthfulness of the contents. The volume offers 'oeuvres de jeunesse ... coups d'essai,' beginning with a translation of Virgil's first eclogue made 'en grande jeunesse' (+2–2v; see also 1958 ed 13–14). Beza's poems were first published in 1548, when their author was nearly thirty: in an undated edition probably of 1550 they are entitled *Poemata juvenilia*, and it is as *Juvenilia* that they are commonly known. In his dedicatory epistle Beza expresses his hesitations about publishing these familiar verses, saying that he finally gathered them together encouraged by the advice of a valued friend. Both volumes consist of different types of verse, such as Complaints, Epitaphs, Ballades, Songs, Epigrams, each set identified by running titles. Marot's volume also contains 'Le Temple de Cupido,' to which 'Cupido Conquered' might be considered a counterblast. Both authors were prominent in the Protestant movement of religious reform. Although Marot for political reasons may have wavered in his professed commitment, he suffered exile for his beliefs, and the translations he made in the 1530s of forty-nine of the psalms were combined with the translations of Beza to form the immensely influential Geneva Psalter (1562). Googe's close connections with the returning Marian exiles argue strongly for his acquaintance with the works of these eminent literary figures of the Protestant reform movement. The probability is increased by the appearance of translations from their poems in Tottel's *Miscellany*: one translation and some smaller borrowings from Marot, and eleven translations from Beza, nine of them by Grimald (Prescott 9–10; Tottel 2:88 etc).

Whether or not Googe and his printer Colwell were influenced by the make-up of Beza's or Marot's publications, the volume they produced, like these continental models, presents clearly defined types of poems, identified by running titles. There are four types: eight Eclogues, four Epitaphs, thirty-six 'Sonnets' (five of them by other hands), and the 'Dream,' 'Cupido Conquered'; two prefatory poems and two prose epistles complete the volume. The collection is unified by its major theme, the exploration of the ways reason should govern the passions, particularly love, and by the prevailing tone of conversation in a close-knit society. However, the evolution of and influences on each type of poem vary.

The main concern of the Eclogues is to explore the problems and dangers of love, through dialogue between older and younger shepherds, through narratives of the unhappy experiences of Dametas,

Faustus, and Selvagia, and through the contrast of human and divine love. References to the zodiac, to the seasons, and to the flocks give pastoral colour, and the contrast between country and town allows for an examination of contemporary religious problems. Several influences are at work in these poems. Most dominant and pervasive is Mantuan, whose *Bucolica* or *Adolescentia* of 1498 was probably known to every schoolboy (not only those taught by Holofernes) for two centuries. The Carmelite friar's moralistic tone informs the first four and the last of Googe's eclogues in particular, although as W.P. Mustard notes, 'there is very little verbal imitation or borrowing in detail' (in Mantuan *Eclogues* 50). Another favourite school author, of a very different persuasion, whose influence is particularly evident in the second and sixth eclogues, is Ovid. His *Remedia amoris* is an obvious source for Googe's argument, but reminiscences of the amatory letters, the *Heroides,* show that Googe did not confine his reading to the anti-erotic. Virgil's *Eclogues* provide many of the pastoral names, and suggestions for Googe's second eclogue. Palingenius's *Zodiacus vitae* contributes to the descriptive seasonal settings of the eclogues, and reinforces their didactic and reformist tone. The lineaments of late medieval moral allegory and morality plays can also be discerned in the eighth eclogue. The influence of other school texts and of modern moralistic literature emerges in the reminiscences of Seneca in the fifth eclogue and of *The Mirror for Magistrates* in the fourth. These influences are fairly homogeneous, since even the pagan and urbane Ovid had been thoroughly moralized into a veneer of respectability over the centuries. The alien influence comes from a source much more recognizably 'renaissance' than 'medieval,' the Spanish pastoral romance, Montemayor's *Diana,* which was an immediate and fashionable success in Europe upon its appearance in 1559. The fifth and seventh eclogues are drawn, by paraphrase and translation, from *Diana,* though Googe has made some significant alterations, particularly in the fifth eclogue. Googe has taken from Montemayor a good story and a lively debate that fit, with a little tailoring, into his condemnation of ungoverned passion. He has not borrowed Montemayor's elegance, or finely wrought song. The singing shepherds moving through European literature from Sannazaro's *Arcadia* emerged naturally by the end of the century into pastoral opera – but not in England. Only one of Montemayor's songs makes its way into Googe's 'sonnets'; even remeasured to a popular song, 'To the Tune of Appelles' retains some of its foreign sparkle. Helen Cooper amusingly criticises Googe for 'seeming to damn a swain who has stepped out of the Italian poetic imagination for not being a Protestant with a keen sense of psychomachia' (125), but it is equally wrong to damn Googe for not achieving what he did not attempt. Like his own Amintas, he does not profess to 'sing in verses sweet,' but claims only 'In simple song I will address / myself, to show my mind' (5.39–40). In the eclogues that youthful, lively mind is expressed with a directness and energy which, if sometimes prosaic, are nearly always engaging.

The main influence on Googe's epitaphs and 'sonnets' comes from his way of life: from his family, his friends, his mentors, his education. The forms he chooses are mainly those of Tottel's *Miscellany*; the poetic methods are those inculcated by school exercises in rhetoric and composition. What is remarkable under these circumstances is how often he achieves a distinctive voice. The four epitaphs celebrate the twin ideals of the renaissance man, martial courage and intellectual accomplishment. All have a tone of intense engagement, though it is unlikely that Googe knew personally Sheffield and Shelley who died when he was a child. The sense of involvement comes more from Googe's response to the ideas that the four men celebrated represent. The encomia to the venerable scholars Alexander Nowell and John Bale, and 'Of Edwards of the Chapel,' are distinguished by a lightness of touch surprising in so young a man addressing his seniors but are nevertheless delightfully warm. The same charmingly personal note informs the poems addressed to friends, particularly the five sets of answer poems exchanged with Blundeston and Neville. The poems are sometimes obviously occasional, such as 'To Mistress D.,' 'Of the unfortunate choice of His Valentine,' and 'Of Mistress D.S.' Others seem to be exercises on a familiar theme, such as 'To Mistress A.' or 'The uncertainty of Life.' Sometimes familiar themes are vivified by personal application, as in 'To M. Edward Cobham,' or by clever reversal of expectation, as in 'Of Money.' Sometimes a poem is spiced by ironic self-deprecation, as in 'To George Holmedon, of a running head,' or by ironic parody, as in 'Out of sight, out of mind.'

The final sequence of 'sonnets,' from 'Going towards Spain,' differs from the rest in that at least four of the six poems were very likely written after Blundeston had sent Googe's earlier collected poems to the printer. The three travel poems could have been inspired by Wyatt's analogous poems, but it would be unreasonable not to suppose that they were also prompted by Googe's own voyage to Spain. The exchange of poems with Blundeston differs from earlier pairs in the use of extended anecdotes from natural history, rather in the manner of the emblem books already popular on the Continent, and the final poem, a translation from Montemayor's *Diana*, sounds a new note of the lyricism of renaissance pastoral romance.

It is the more surprising to find the very next poem, 'Cupido Conquered,' the last and longest in the volume, at first sight thoroughly medieval, a concoction of Chaucer and Prudentius with a dollop of Ovid and a sprinkle of Surrey. But there is also a colouring of Montemayor, and the influence of Chaucer is important in the way that he spoke to the Renaissance, as great poets speak directly to each age as well as for their own. The direction of Googe's poem is not to the culling of the rose, but to the conquest of love, and the vision of this triumph is given to the poet by the Muses as a reward for his efforts. The strongest Chaucerian influence comes from the dreamer of *The House of Fame*, preoccupied with the nature of poetic fame, and the dreamer of *The Parliament of Fowls*, seeking to understand the nature of love and restlessly dissatisfied with visions of passionate desire or natural inclination. Googe's hastily finished experiment suffers by comparison with the mature work of a great poet, but on its own terms it is sufficiently accomplished to be entertaining, and it provides an interesting example of the possibilities of old forms as vehicles for new ideas.

The form of Googe's verse, particularly its metre, has sometimes proved a barrier to the enjoyment of the poetry. He writes in very regular iambics, sometimes in fourteeners, sometimes in poulter's measure, sometimes pentameter, occasionally tetrameter. The fourteeners and poulter's measure of course rhyme in couplets. Except for two poems in stanzas ('Out of sight, out of mind' and 'To the Tune of Apelles'), all poems in pentameter and tetrameter are cross-rhymed, usually with a concluding couplet. This last habit, when the poem is fourteen lines long, results in a form like an English sonnet. Googe's use of 'sonnet' to describe all his short poems other than the epitaphs is cited by the *Oxford English Dictionary* as the first example of such usage, though it is conceded that the 'sonnets' of the title of Tottel's *Miscellany* may also embrace this meaning. Clearly Googe did not consider 'sonnet' a limited technical term, and it seems unlikely that he is deliberately using the form in 'To George Holmedon' or 'Unhappy tongue.' He shows no interest in experimenting with metrical forms, either in emulating varied lyrical measures of the medieval English and French tradition, or in exploring the wealth of metres in Montemayor's *Diana*. His metrical aim seems always to be to achieve smoothness, perhaps what Neville meant in praising his 'pleasant framèd style' or Blundeston his 'filèd work' and 'comely grace.' It is hard for many modern readers to overcome a dislike of the long trot of the fourteener, although Ezra Pound called it a 'pleasing and popular measure' (227) and T.S. Eliot claimed for it 'undeniable poetic charms' (in Seneca *Tenne Tragedies* xxxi). Its regular beat, and the smoothed-out rhythms of other line-lengths in Tottel's edition, give rise to a common complaint against mid-Tudor verse, that it is monotonous and rigid. G.K. Hunter suggests that 'the rigidity of these meters may have a moral as well as a metrical aspect. It is not hard to imagine their attraction for the moralist who is stressing above all things the common lot that holds individual egotism in check' (10). The purposefulness of Googe's metrical rhythms may be discerned by comparing the frequently inverted syntax of his verse with his prose, which is elegantly wrought and harmonious but not syntactically inverted. Since Googe himself contrasts 'the plain and smooth style' of prose with 'the haughty and heavenly style' of verse, it would seem that he considers that the artificial moulding of the language to the metrical beat adds to the elevation and force of verse, which with 'sugared sentences' and 'thundering words' assaults and exiles vice (p 133).

Googe was a thoughtful, intelligent, and by 1561, a practised writer. But he was also a very young one. Most of the verse in the 1563 volume was written before he left England for Spain in the autumn of 1561, when he was just twenty-one. Some of it, particularly the eclogues most influenced by Mantuan, may well have been written several years earlier. One of the chief pleasures offered by these 'juvenilia' or 'adolescentia' is their engaging combination of youthful earnestness and high spirits.

Even before he was twenty, Googe's translation of Palingenius won for him immediate and continuing praise. References to him as an original poet are much fewer. In an anti-papist poem by Richard Robinson, *The Reward of Wickedness* (?1574), written during his turns of duty guarding the captive Mary, Queen of Scots, the author is given a vision of Mount Helicon. Here he sees portraits of 'all the Poets,' Homer, Virgil, Ovid, Chaucer, and many more 'too long to name.' Looking round to see if any of his countrymen are there, he espies 'Skelton and Lydgate, / Wager, Heywood, and Barnabe Googe, all these together sat / With divers other English men, whose names I will omit' (Q2v). This oddity carries little weight as a critical estimate. It is more impressive when Gabriel Harvey, surveying the literary scene from Grafton and Heywood to Daniel and Southwell, places Googe among those 'vulgar writers' in whom 'many things are commendable, divers things notable, some things excellent' (*Works* 2:290).

In this century Googe has won praise for his contribution to the development of the English eclogue, and as a lyricist, but not always from the same critics for both kinds of verses. The influential W.W. Greg and E.A. Greenlaw both find his eclogues worth attention, the latter placing them at the head of the native influences that are 'of great importance' to an understanding of Spenser's *Shepheardes Calender* (Greg 80–2; Greenlaw 424–8, 446). In more recent years his eclogues have continued to find some favour with writers on pastoral, and it is his third eclogue which opens *The Penguin Book of English Pastoral Verse* (1975).

The single work which probably did most to give Googe status as a lyric poet in the twentieth century is Yvor Winters' 'The 16th Century Lyric in England,' where he takes 'Of Money' as representative of the qualities that he considers characteristic of the best tradition of the English lyric (96). Other critics, such as Alan Stephens, John Williams, Douglas Peterson, and Richard Panofsky, have developed this line of criticism, even sometimes overgoing Winters, to find 'Of Money' 'rather complex,' 'nicely ironic,' 'wry, cynical, just a bit audacious' (Webster 33). Googe has also been fortunate in having two good studies totally devoted to his life and work: the 1954 unpublished Harvard dissertation of Brooke Peirce, and the 1981 volume by William Sheidley in Twayne's English Authors Series. Both provide thorough, well-balanced views of Googe's achievement, helping to make it possible for Googe to benefit from Gabriel Harvey's injunction: 'Let every man in his degree enjoy his due' (*Works* 2:290).

Editorial Practice

This modernized edition of Googe's *Eclogues, Epitaphs, and Sonnets* (1563) is based on the copy in the Henry E. Huntington Library of San Marino, California. Discussion relating to the establishment of an accurate text, and to textual and bibliographical problems of the volume, may be found in the Textual Appendix.

The chief aspects of the text affected by the process of modernization are typography, punctuation, spelling, and lineation.

The use of long s, u/v, i/j has been normalized; tildes, ampersands, and contracted forms (for example w, y) have been silently expanded. Running titles and catchwords have been ignored. Italicization of proper names has been abandoned. Capitalization has been reduced to proper nouns. Some interesting effects of semi-personification (for example in the first eclogue, liberty, bondage, affection, wit, fancy, hope, presence) are given less emphasis as a result, but capitalization in the text is so frequent and so inconsistent that it is distracting to most modern readers. An exception is made for Love, when it refers to the god (decisions on this point are often debatable), and for the personifications in Blundeston's 'Preface' and in 'Cupido Conquered.' Titles of poems are capitalized according to the practice of the 1563 edition.

Punctuation has been arbitrarily imposed according to the taste of the editor. The 1563 punctuation is very heavy, and does not seem to yield consistent patterns of usage: sometimes punctuation is inserted in the middle or at the end of the line without any regard for sense, breaking up the predicate or separating adjective from pronoun.[13] In setting off the vocative, parentheses have been replaced by commas.

Choices in modernizing spelling present many difficulties: for example, in this edition, the archaic form *seely* has been retained, because the modern spelling *silly* can be very misleading. When two possibilities make equally good sense, as for example *altogether* or *all together* at line 22 of the epistle to Lovelace, a note is provided in the Commentary. Spellings involving elisions, contractions, and inflected endings are of special importance because they affect metrical regularity and sometimes indicate colloquial speech. Where modernized spelling of a form alters syllable count, compression is indicated by replacing the expected letter with an apostrophe (for example, thickst = thick'st; needst = need'st). Shortened preterite or past participle forms are expanded silently when this involves no change in the number of syllables (for example, discoverd = discovered). When it is necessary to sound the ending, the syllable is marked (as in *condemnèd*). Sometimes words occur in both contracted and uncontracted forms, and the spelling does not always accurately indicate which form should be used: for instance, *countenance*, *enemy*, *never*, and other words containing a *v* between vowels, such as *whatsoever*[14]; these contractions are not marked in the text. Elisions are sometimes indicated in the original spelling and these are expanded with an apostrophe: for example, thother = th'other. However, elisions are often not indicated by the original spelling, and these have not been marked in the modernized text: some examples are *though it* (original spelling *thoo it*) (5.153), *the unjust* (9.96), *to obey* (10.81), *guilty of* (11.78). There is a particularly interesting group of contracted forms in the seventh eclogue, indicating colloquial speech. Some of them are indicated in the 1563 text, and are normally modernized (tys = 'tis, Its = It's, whats = what's), but some contractions of noun or pronoun with verb are not marked in the 1563 text, readers being evidently expected to make them naturally. For example, *he is*, *woman is*, *they are*, *you have* (11.93, 97, 186, 198) should be read 'he's,' 'woman's,' 'they're,' 'you've'; similarly at 48.455 *he will* reads 'he'll'. In all cases whether or not a form is to be contracted or elided can be determined by the syllable count.[15]

One other formal characteristic affected by modernization needs comment: lineation. In the body of the 1563 volume, all but three poems are printed in broken lines. (The three exceptions are 'The Answer of A. Neville to the same,' 'Out of sight, out of mind,' and 'To the Tune of Appelles;' all three of these are octosyllabic, and the last two are the only poems by Googe in stanzas.) It is very common in the sixteenth century for lines of sixteen, fourteen, and twelve syllables to be printed or written divided. As often noted, when divided the fourteener may be taken as ballad or common measure, and is often found written stanzaically in manuscript. Googe seems to have considered the question of whether his fourteeners were printed broken or not a matter of indifference: his translation of Palingenius is printed in broken lines in 1560, 1561, and 1565, but in long lines in 1576 and 1588. In the *Eclogues, Epitaphs, and Sonnets* of 1563, the second half of the line of Googe's fourteeners and poulter's measure is normally indented, and not capitalized, but the second half of Neville's fourteeners in the two poems both titled 'Alexander Neville's Answer to the same' is usually capitalized. This distinction perhaps indicates that Googe wrote his fourteeners unbroken, and Neville broken. However, since Googe was obviously quite content to have his fourteeners printed broken and since both methods of presentation were equally acceptable and familiar in Googe's day, I have followed my own preference in this edition by printing fourteeners and poulter's measure in broken lines, with the second half indented and not capitalized. The lineation of these longer verses is commonplace, but the breaking of pentameter and even tetrameter is odd, and has given rise to some comment.[16] One reason for this breaking is obvious: pentameter would not fit on the page, even the eight-syllable half-line often awkwardly needing to have a word or two bracketed below, but this practical consideration does not explain the breaking of the tetrameter of 'To M. Henry Cobham of the most blessed state of Life.' The printer has signalled his awareness of the difference between the tetrameter and pentameter on the one hand, and poulter's measure and fourteeners on the other, by not indenting the second half of the shorter lines. The lack of experience in breaking the lines is also shown in some irregularities in the pattern of four and four, or four and six. In one instance, such an irregularity has been corrected during printing (in 'The Answer of L. Blundeston to the same'). Despite the interesting effects that might be considered to arise from this breaking, it seems likely that both author and printer thought of the lines as whole, and they are here printed unbroken. The Commentary notes poems that have had their lineation altered, and lists irregularities in the 1563 breaking.

Notes

Parenthetical references to Googe's poems are to the numbers in this edition. Full bibliographical information is provided in the list of Works Cited, pp 203–12.

1 Much of the following account relies on the original biographical research in Peirce, supplemented by Pinkerton, Sheidley (1981), and Eccles.

2 The *Zodiacus vitae* of Marcellus Palingenius Stellatus was a school text in sixteenth-century England (see Baldwin, passim). Googe published his translation in three stages: the first three books in 1560, the first six books in 1561, and the whole twelve in 1565. A revised edition appeared in 1576; this has been issued in facsimile (1947) with prefatory matter from the other editions and an excellent introduction by Rosemond Tuve.

3 Phrases from the 1560, 1561, and 1565 title-pages and from the dedicatory epistle to Lady Hales.

4 By Nilus Cabasilas, translated by Thomas Gressop. It was entered in the Stationers' Register 16 March 1560, and published by Ralph Newbery, the publisher of Googe's translation of Palingenius as well as of the *Eclogues, Epitaphs, and Sonnets*; see Textual Appendix.

5 Lambarde 58–63. Gilbert Duke, who wrote commendatory verses for the 1560 Palingenius, George Holmedon of 'To George Holmedon of a running Head' (26), and Edward Dering, who contributed commendatory Latin verses to the 1561 Palingenius, are perhaps related to the Thomas Duke, William Holmden, and Richard Deering of Lambarde's list. The names of Edward Dering (Edouardus Deering) and of Googe's cousin Alexander Neville appear among the Kentish writers added by Lambarde to the list drawn from Bale's compilation (66). Googe is not listed. Dering was the same age as Googe, and a contemporary at Christ's College, Cambridge, but his interests were more exclusively theological (see DNB 5:843–5).

6 McKisack 49; she is quoting Strype who in turn is paraphrasing Neville.

7 See DNB 6:1–2. See also Spenser's letter to Harvey (*Poetical Works* 612) and Ringler (in Sidney *Poems* 390–2).

8 Ariosto 435: the note gives Neville higher marks than King James VI. In the same set of annotations to the thirty-seventh book Harington praises Lady Burleigh and her sisters.

9 Neville's brother Thomas also had connections with the Sidney and Spenser circles, but less amicable ones. He was in 1573 'a malevolent enemy' to Spenser's close friend Gabriel Harvey and made a spirited though eventually unsuccessful attempt to ruin Harvey's career by blocking the award of his MA degree at Cambridge (Stern 16). However, this malice of Googe's cousin did not prevent Harvey in 1598 from praising the gentleman 'that bestowed an English livery' on Palingenius, as one who had not 'wronged' his author (*Marginalia* 231).

10 Sheidley (1981) 124. Some of the emotions in the dispute were perhaps heightened by religious differences. The Darrells favoured Catholicism, and in the 1590s their Scotney home figured in an exciting Jesuit concealment and escape (Morey 195–6). But Mary seems to have been happy to live in the Anglican way. Her rejected suitor did not suffer long, making a marriage probably much more appealing to his rich father. His wife was the sister of the tenth Baron Dacre of the South, who upon her brother's death in 1594 successfully claimed his title and entailed estates (see the article on Fiennes or Fienes, Gregory in DNB 6:1292).

11 Among the members of the dinner party was Nicasius Yetswaert, who is named in the list of English 'authorities' added by Googe to his translation of Heresbach's *Four Books of Husbandry* (1577). Peirce speculates on a connection with the Jacob Itzuert who contributes a Latin poem to the 1565 Palingenius.

12 Edward de Vere, seventeenth Earl of Oxford, 1550–1604, became a ward of the Court on his father's death in 1562. He was himself a noted poet and patron, but suffered from what the DNB understatedly calls 'a waywardness of temper' that led to the fatal wounding of an undercook at Cecil House and that made him a most unsatisfactory son-in-law when he married Cecil's daughter Anne (DNB 20:225–34).

13 One rather interesting practice in punctuation not reproduced here is the placing of the question mark between the main and dependent clauses: for example in the seventh eclogue, ll.55–6 'What chance hast thou? that thus thou hast / Syrenus sweet forlorn.'

14 Medial v seems particularly to afford opportunity for flexibility. Compare for example, Spenser: *never* is disyllabic in the August eclogue of *The Shepheardes Calender* at line 20 and monosyllabic at line 50; *ever* is disyllabic in the December eclogue at line 30 and monosyllabic at line 112;

even is disyllabic in *The Faerie Queene* at VI vii 36.4 and monosyllabic at VI vii 1.3. Harvey apparently thought that words with *v* between vowels should regularly be monosyllabic (*Marginalia* 168–9).

15 Problems of modernization affecting spelling, punctuation, and metre have been discussed in full and lively fashion by Stanley Wells in his monograph *Modernizing Shakespeare's Spelling*. It is his opinion that stress is more important than syllable count in determining the uniformity or consistency of Shakespeare's metre (22–3). In Googe's verse, although the stress rhythm is very clear (sometimes painfully so), the syllable count is the determining factor, and governs pronunciation.

16 For example, Saintsbury 323–4; Hudson 293–4; Lewis 259; Thompson 67–9. Thompson likes the effect of the broken lines, which he analyses in a passage from 'An Epitaph of the Death of Nicholas Grimald.' A comment he makes on p 62 suggests that Turbervile also broke pentameter lines, but a check of Turbervile's *Epigrams, Epitaphs, Songs and Sonnets* (1567) and Thompson's own table of Stanza Forms (157–8) shows only one poem of lines shorter than twelve syllables printed broken (other than Googe's), and that is a single pentameter couplet by Turbervile 'Againe of Drunkennesse,' whose large ornamental capital encourages the breaking of the line.

TEXTS

Eglogs

Epytaphes, and *Sonettes*.
Newly written by
Barnabe Googe:

1563.

15. Marche.

¶ Imprynted at London, by
Thomas Colwell, for Raffe
Newbery, dwelyng in
Fleetstrete a litle a-
boue the Conduit
in the late shop
of Thomas
Bartelet.

B.Googe.

Alexander Neville.

The mountains high the blust'ring winds,
the floods the rocks withstand,
The cities strong the cannon's shot
and threat'ning chieftain's hand,
The castles huge by long besiege
and dreadful battery brook
Both fire and flames and thund'ring thumps,
and every deadly stroke
With fervent broiling furious rage
doth beat and drive to ground
The long defencèd walls by force
and throughly them confound:
Right so thy muse, O worthy Googe,
thy pleasant framèd style,
Discovered lies to momish mouths,
reproachful tongues, and vile
Defaming minds. Regard them not.
Press thou for higher praise.
Submit thyself to persons grave,
whose judgement right always
By reason ruled doth rightly judge,
whom fancies none can charm,
Which in the most inconstant brains
are chiefly wont to swarm,
Whom no desire of filthy gain,
whom lucre none can move
From truth to stray. Such men esteem,
such, such, embrace and love.

On such men stay thy tender years;
such patrons seek to choose,
Which taught by time and practised proof
uprightest judgement use.
But as for those crabsnouted beasts,
those raging fiends of hell,
Whose vile, malicious, hateful minds
with boiling rancour swell,
Which puffed with pride, enflamed with spite,
and drowned in deep disdain,
Like Momus' monstrous brood outright
even of a jealous brain,
With curious, cankered, carping mouths
most famous deeds defame,
Defacing those whose labours great
deserve immortal name;
Such crabfaced, cankered, carlish chuffs,
within whose hateful breasts
Such malice bides, such rancour broils,
such endless envy rests,
Esteem thou not. No prejudice
to thee: nor yet opprest
Thy famous writings are by them.
Thou livest and ever shalt.
Not all the sland'ring tongues alive
may purchase blame or fault
Unto thy name, O worthy Googe;
no time, no fiery flame,
Not all the Furies' fretting force
thy doings may defame.
Let them in broil of burning spite
continual toil sustain,
Let them feel scourging plagues of mind,
let ever-during pain
Spread through their poisoned veins. Let care
with peise of deadly weight
Oppress their vile infected hearts,
with stinging malice freight.
Let them destroy themselves in time,
in rancour let them boil:

Let mortal hate, let pinching grief,
    let flaming torments broil
Within their grievous vexèd breasts
    for evermore to dwell:
Let them feel envy's cursèd force,
    (consuming fiend of hell).
Defy them all. *Misanthropoi*
    and squint-eyed monsters right
They are. In fine, leave sow to swill
    and chuff to cankered spite.
But thou proceed in virtuous deeds,
    and as thou hast begun,
Go forward still to advance thy fame.
    Life's race half rightly run
Far easier 'tis for to obtain
    the Type of true renown.
Like labours have been recompensed
    with an immortal crown.
By this doth famous Chaucer live,
    by this a thousand more
Of later years. By this alone
    the old renownèd store
Of ancient poets live. By this
    their praise aloft doth mount
Unto the skies, and equal is
    with stars above. Account
Thyself then worthy of the like,
    if that thou dost proceed
By famous deeds thy fame to enhance
    and name abroad to spread.
With courage stout then through the thick'st
    thou need'st not for to fear:
Not he that saith, but he that doth,
    ought glory's garland wear.
Thus shalt thou still augment thy name,
    and win thee high renown,
And present praise in present life,
    and after death a crown
Of honour, that forever lasts:
    immortal fame, in fine.

To whose reward, thy faithful friend
doth wholly thee resign.
Finis

2

To the right worshipful
M. William Lovelace, Esquire,
Reader of Gray's Inn:
Barnabe Googe wisheth health.

How loath I have been, being of long time earnestly required to suffer these trifles of mine to come to light, it is not unknown to a great number of my familiar acquaintance, who both daily and hourly moved me thereunto and little of long time prevailed therein. For I both considered and weighed with myself the grossness of my style, which thus committed to the gazing show of every eye should forthwith disclose the manifest folly of the writer; and also I feared and mistrusted the disdainful minds of a number both scornful and carping correctors whose heads are ever busied in taunting judgements, lest they should otherwise interpret my doings than indeed I meant them. These two so great mischiefs utterly dissuaded me from the following of my friends' persuasions, and willed me rather to condemn them to continual darkness whereby no inconvenience could happen, than to endanger myself in giving them to light to the disdainful doom of any offended mind. Notwithstanding, all the diligence that I could use in the suppression thereof could not suffice; for I myself being at that time out of the realm, little fearing any such thing to happen, a very friend of mine, bearing as it seemed better will to my doings than respecting the hazard of my name, committed them all together unpolished to the hands of the printer, in whose hands during his absence from the city till his return of late they remained. At which time, he declared the matter wholly unto me; showing me, that being so far past, and paper provided for the impression thereof, it could not without great hindrance of the poor printer be now revoked. His sudden tale made me at the first utterly amazed, and doubting a great while, what was best to be done; at the length agreeing both with necessity and his counsel, I said with Martial: *iam sed poteras tutior esse domi*. And calling to mind to whom I might chiefly commit the fruits of my smiling muse, suddenly was cast before my eyes the perfect view of your friendly mind, gentle Master Lovelace; unto whom for the numbered heaps of sundry friendships accounting myself as bound, I have thought best to give them, not doubting but that they shall be as well taken as I do presently mean them.

Desiring you herein, as all such as shall read them, especially to bear with the unpleasant form of my too hastily finished Dream, the greater part whereof with little advice I lately ended, because the beginning of it, as a senseless head separated from the body, was given with the rest to be printed. And thus desiring but for recompense the friendly receiving of my slender gift, I end: wishing unto you good Master Lovelace, in this life the happy enjoying of prosperous years, and hereafter the blessed estate of never ceasing joy.

Yours assuredly
Barnabe Googe.

*3 L. Blundeston to the Reader.

To creep into thy favour, good Reader, with a long painted preamble in praise of this author, I account it as vain. The sunbeams gives light sufficient. To move thy affection with forepromised pleasure in reading the volume, I think it as bootless. Gold is of self-force and virtue to draw the desire. But with flowers of rhetoric first to delight thee, or with pithy reasons to win thy good will and friendly report for this my attempt; – if such tropes and signs were flowing in me to persuade well thy favour or so much discretion wanting in thee to neglect my good meaning, I would either enforce myself to use a better kind of persuasion or else withdraw my good will from the sentence of so carping and slender a judgement. But as I have felt no floods of the one, so likewise I see no ebbs of the other, that if I were no more barren of the first than fearful of the last, I would be then no more sparing to horde up my treasure from thee than I trust to find thee thankful now in taking this present from me; which not only to show my goodwill (as my Preface discourseth more largely) by preserving the worthy fame and memory of my dear friend M. Googe in his absence, I have presumed more boldly to hazard the printing hereof, though this may suffice to excuse well my enterprise, but also to stir up thy pleasure and further thy profit by reading these his works, which here I have published openly unto thee. And so, being unstored myself, I seek to satisfy thy learned or willing desire with other men's travails. But where the power faileth the will may suffice; the giver, not the gift, is to be regarded; prefer Colonus' radish root before the courtier's barbed horse.

Accept my goodwill and weigh not the value; so shalt thou bind me, if power (as it is unlikely) may answer hereafter my meaning, to gratify thee with the whole fruits of mine own endeavour: and so shalt thou encourage others to make thee partaker of the like or far greater jewels, who yet doubting thy unthankful receipt niggardly keep them to their own use and private commodity, whereas being assured of the contrary by thy friendly report of other men's travails, they could perhaps be easily entreated more freely to lend them abroad to thy greater avail and furtherance. Thus therefore to thy good or evil taking I put forth this pattern for others to follow in weightier matters or else to beware by other men's harms, in keeping their names unreproved by silence.

From my chamber,
the xxvii of May,
1562.

*4 The Preface of L. Blundeston.

The senses dull of my appallèd muse,
Forwearied with the travail of my brain
In scanning of the argued books diffuse,
And dark for me the glimmering sight to gain,
Debated long what exercise to use,
To file the edgeless parts of wit again,
To cleanse the head from sleepy humours' slime,
To rouse the heart from drowsy dreams in time.

The mind desires to break from thoughtful den
And time requires the painted fields to view.
The eye procures to please the fancy then
With fieldish sights of divers colours new.
The smelling likes the savour sweet of them;
The ear agrees the pleasant lay anew

Of birds to hear. Thus these do all contrive
With this disport the spirits to revive.

But Fancy then, by search of self-device,
Renouncing thus to spend the pleasant May
So vainly out with sport of fruitless price,
Found out at length this practice for my play,
To pen in verse the toys of her device
To pass this time of Pentecost away;
Whose idle days she willed me thus to spend
And publish forth her doings in the end.

Quod Reason, 'No,' and brake, her tale begun,
'Wilt thou presume, like Bayard blind, to press
'Into the throng of all the lookers-on,
'Whose viewing eyes will weigh thy wisdom less
'To see the thread of all thy works ill-spun
'Drawn out at length unto the common guess,
'Than if thou shouldst keep to thyself thy clew
'Where none thy works besides thyself may view.'

With this rose up from out her seat behind
Dame Memory, and Reason thus besought:
'Since, Lady, chief of us thou art assigned
'To rule and temper all my secret thought
'And to restrain affections' fancy blind,
'Let me entreat, if I may pierce thee ought,
'For to present a solace very fit
'Our senses dull with changèd muse to whet.

'Lo here the eye a paper bunch doth see
'Of filèd work of Googe's flowing head,
'Left here behind, when hence he passed from me,
'In all the storms that winter blasts bespread,
'Through swelling seas and lofty mountains high
'Of Pyrenei the paths unknown to tread.
'Whose great good will I keep, and in his place
'His verses crave to represent his face.

'Unfold the truss therefore, and if the Muse
'Be sotted so with this grave study past
'In so short space, or if we seek to choose

'To print our acts in safety at the last.
'Cease of a while this labour and peruse
'These papers left of such delighting taste,
'And put in print these works of worthy skill.
'So shall we show the fruits of our good will.'

This Fancy liked, imagining aright
Of her own joy in hearing of his verse
And pleasant style most pithily indite,
Whose fame forth blown, his deeds could well rehearse.
But for to paint my name in open sight
With others' stuff, this would she fain reverse,
And thinks I should in others' plumes so show
Myself, to be a second Aesop's crow.

But after, when the eye had viewed each line
That Googe had penned and left behind with me,
When Memory could all the effect resign
To Reason's skill to weigh them as they lie
With long rehearse of trièd faith by time,
Then Fancy soon her pride began to ply,
And all received much pleasure to the mind,
More profit far than Fancy had assigned.

And Fancy thus herself with blushing face,
Condemnèd by Dame Reason's doom divine
To see th'alluring style, the comely grace,
The sappy sense of this his passing rhyme,
So far surmounting her invention base,
And hearing of his friendliness in fine,
Which Memory her storehouse held full fast,
Allowèd well their judgements at the last.

Since every sense did wonted strength renew, –
The blood congealed, recoursèd to his place;
The wits benumbed brought to their proper cue;
The heart oppressed with old delighting grace
Unburdened now and puffed with pleasure new
By taking of this book the viewing gaze, –
They all at once Goodwill now called upon
To wrest herself to quite these works anon.

Thus pushed I forth straight to the printer's hand
These Eclogues, Sonnets, Epitaphs of men,
Unto the reader's eyes for to be scanned,
With praises such as is due unto them;
Who absent now their Master may commend
And feed his fame whatsoever faileth him.
Give Googe therefore his own deservèd fame;
Give Blundeston leave to wish well to his name.
Finis.

Daphnes. Amintas.

ECLOGUES

5 Egloga prima.
[The First Eclogue.]

Daphnes *Amintas*

Sith Phoebus now begins to flame,
O friend Amintas dear,
And placèd hath his gorgeous globe
in midst of all the sphere,
And from that place doth cast his beams
where (they that stars define)
Lies point (do say) that termèd is
right equinoctial line,
Whereas the Ram doth cause to spring
each herb and flower in field,
And forceth ground, that spoiled of green
did lie, new green to yield,
Let shepherds us yield also tales,
as best becomes the time:
Such tales as winter storms have stayed
in country poets' rhyme.
Begin to sing, Amintas, thou:
for why? thy wit is best,
And many a sagèd saw lies hid
within thine agèd breast.
Oft have I heard, of shepherds old,
thy fame reported true;
No herdman lives, but knows the praise
to old Amintas due.
Begin therefore, and I give ear,

for talk doth me delight.
Go, boy; go drive the beasts to feed
while he his mind recite.

Amintas Thy praises, Daphnes, are too great,
and more for me than meet;
Nor ever I such sagèd saws
could sing in verses sweet.
And now to talk of springtime tales
my hairs too hoar do grow;
Such tales as these I told in time
when youthful years did flow.
But since, I cannot thee deny,
thy father's love doth bind,
In simple song I will address
myself, to show my mind.
Long hast thou, Daphnes, me required
the state of love to tell,
For in my youth I knew the force
and passions all full well.
Now love therefore I will define
and what it is declare,
Which way poor souls it doth entrap
and how it them doth snare.
My boy, remove my beasts from hence
and drive them farther down;
Upon the hills let them go feed
that join to yonder town.
O Cupid, king of fiery love,
aid thou my singing verse,
And teach me here the cause and case
of lovers to rehearse.
Direct my tongue in troth to tread,
with fury fill my brain,
That I may able be to tell
the cause of lovers' pain.
Opinions divers could I show,
but chiefest of them all
I will declare, and for the rest
with silence leave I shall.
A fervent humour (some do judge)
within the head doth lie,

Which issuing forth with poisoned beams
    doth run from eye to eye,
And taking place abroad in heads
    a while doth firmly rest
Till frenzy framed in fancy fond
    descends from head to breast,
And poison strong from eyes outdrawn   Plato
    doth pierce the wretched heart,
And all infects the blood about
    and boils in every part.
Thus when the beams infected hath
    the woeful lovers' blood,
The senses all do straight decay,
    oppressed with fury's flood.
Then liberty withdraws herself
    and bondage bears the sway,
Affection blind then leads the heart
    and wit is wound away.
O Daphnes, then the pains appear
    and torments all of hell.
Then seeks the seely wounded soul
    the flames for to expel.
But all too late, alas, he strives,
    for fancy bears the stroke,
And he must toil (no help there is)
    in slavish servile yoke.
His blood corrupted all within
    doth boil in every vein:
Then seeks he how to sue for salve
    that may redress his pain.
And when the face he doth behold
    by which he should have aid
And sees no help, then looks he long
    and trembleth all afraid,
And museth at the framèd shape
    that hath his life in hands.
Now fast he flies about the flames,
    now still amazèd stands.
Yet hope relieves his hurtful heat,
    and will doth pain make light;
And all the griefs that then he feels

doth presence still requite.
But when the light absented is
and beams in heart remain,
Then flames the fire fresh again
and new begins his pain.
Then long he looks his loss to see,
then sobs and sighs abound,
Then mourneth he to miss the mark
that erst too soon he found.
Then shadeful places out he looks,
and all alone he lives,
Exiling joy and mirth from him,
himself to wailing gives,
And still his mind thereon doth muse
and still thereof he prates.
O Daphnes, here I swear to thee,
no grief to lover's state.
If he but once behold the place
where he was wont to meet
The pleasant form that him enflamed,
and joyful countenance sweet,
The place (a wondrous thing I tell)
his grief augmenteth new,
Yet still he seeks the place to see
that most he should eschew.
If but the name rehearsèd be
(a thing more strange to hear),
Then colour comes and goes in haste,
then quaketh he for fear, –
The very name hath such a force
that it can daze the mind
And make the man amazed to stand, –
what force hath love to bind?
Affection none to this is like,
it doth surmount them all.
Of griefs, the greatest grief, no doubt,
is to be Venus' thrall.
And therefore, Daphnes, now beware,
for thou art young and free;
Take heed of viewing faces long
for loss of liberty.

I shall not need (I think) to bid
thee, to detest the crime
Of wicked love that Jove did use Jupiter
in Ganymede's time.
For rather would I (though it be much)
that thou should'st seek the fire
Of lawful love that I have told
than burn with such desire.
And thus an end: I wearied am,
my wind is old and faint,
Such matters I do leave to such
as finer far can paint.
Fetch in the goat that goes astray
and drive him to the fold.
My years be great; I will be gone,
for springtime nights be cold.

Daphnes Great thanks to thee for this thy tale,
Amintas, here I give,
But never can I make amends
to thee whilst I do live.
Yet for thy pains (no recompense)
a small reward have here:
A whistle framèd long ago,
wherewith my father dear
His joyful beasts was wont to keep.
No pipe for tune so sweet
Might shepherd ever yet possess, –
a thing for thee full meet.

Finis Eglogae primae.

6 Egloga secunda.
[The Second Eclogue.]

Dametas

My beasts, go feed upon the plain,
and let your herdman lie.
Thou seest her mind, and fear'st thou now,
Dametas, for to die?
Why stayest thou thus? why dost thou stay?
thy life too long doth last.

Account this flood thy fatal grave
 sith time of hope is past.
What mean'st thou thus to linger on?
 thy life would fain depart:
Alas, the wound doth fester still
 of cursèd Cupid's dart.
No salve but this can help thy sore,
 nothing can move her mind;
She hath decreed, that thou shalt die,
 no help there is to find.
Now sith there is no other help,
 nor ought but this to try,
Thou seest her mind: why fear'st thou then,
 Dametas, for to die?
Long hast thou served, and servèd true,
 but all, alas, in vain,
For she thy service nought esteems
 but deals thee grief for gain.
For thy goodwill, (a gay reward)
 disdain, for love she gives.
Thou lovest her while thy life doth last,
 she hates thee while she lives.
Thou flam'st whenas thou seest her face
 with heat of high desire,
She flames again, but how? alas,
 with deep disdainful ire.
The greatest pleasure is to thee
 to see her void of pain;
The greatest grief to her again
 to see thy health remain.
Thou covet'st ever her to find,
 she seeks from thee to fly;
Thou seest her mind: why fear'st thou then,
 Dametas, for to die?
Dost thou account it best to keep
 thy life in sorrows still?
Or think'st thou best it now to live,
 contrary to her will?
Think'st thou thy life for to retain
 when she is not content?
Canst thou addict thyself to live

and she to murder bent?
Dost thou intend again to sue
for mercy at her hands?
As soon thou may'st go plough the rocks
and reap upon the sands.
Draw near, O mighty herd of beasts,
sith no man else is by,
Your herdman long that hath you kept,
Dametas now must die.
Resolve your brutish eyes to tears
and all together cry,
Bewail the woeful end of love:
Dametas now must die.
My pleasant songs now shall you hear
no more on mountains high.
I leave you all, I must be gone.
Dametas now must die.
To Tityrus I you resign,
in pasture good to lie,
For Tityrus shall keep you, though
Dametas now must die.
O cursèd cause that hath me slain
my troth, alas, to try:
O shepherds all, be witnesses,
Dametas here doth die.
Finis Eglogae secundae.

7 Egloga tertia.
[The Third Eclogue.]

Menalcas *Coridon*

A pleasant weather, Coridon,
and fit to keep the field
This moon hath brought: hear'st thou the birds
what joyful tunes they yield?
Lo, how the lusty lambs do course,
whom springtime heat doth prick.
Behold again, the agèd ewes
with bouncing leaps do kick.
Amongst them all, what ails thy ram

to halt so much behind?
Some sore mischance hath him befall'n,
or else some grief of mind,
For wont he was of stomach stout
and courage high to be,
And lookèd proud amongst the flock,
and none so stout as he.

Coridon A great mishap and grief of mind
is him befall'n of late,
Which causeth him against his will
to lose his old estate.
A lusty flock hath Tityrus
that him Dametas gave,
(Dametas he, that martyr died,
whose soul the heavens have)
And in this flock full many ewes
of pleasant form do go,
With them a mighty ram doth run,
that works all wooers woe.
My ram, when he the pleasant dames
had viewèd round about,
Chose ground of battle with his foe
and thought to fight it out.
But all too weak, alas, he was,
although his heart was good,
For when his enemy him espied
he ran with cruel mood
And with his crookèd weapon smote
him sore upon the side
A blow of force, that stayed not there
but to the legs did glide
And almost lamed the wooer quite
(such haps in love there be).
This is the cause of all his grief
and wailing that you see.

Menalcas Well, Coridon, let him go halt,
and let us both go lie
In yonder bush of juniper;
the beasts shall feed hereby.
A pleasant place here is to talk:
good Coridon, begin,

And let us know the town's estate,
    that thou remainest in.

Coridon The town's estate? Menalcas, O,
    thou mak'st my heart to groan,
For vice hath every place possessed
    and virtue thence is flown.
Pride bears herself as goddess chief
    and boasts above the sky,
And lowliness an abject lies,
    with gentleness her by.
Wit is not joined with simpleness
    as she was wont to be,
But seeks the aid of arrogance
    and crafty policy.
Nobility begins to fade,
    and carters up do spring,
Than which no greater plague can hap
    nor more pernicious thing.
Menalcas, I have known myself,
    within this thirty year,
Of lords and ancient gentlemen
    a hundred dwelling there,
Of whom we shepherds had relief:
    such gentleness of mind
Was placèd in their noble hearts
    as none is now to find.
But haughtiness and proud disdain
    hath now the chief estate,
For Sir John Straw, and Sir John Cur,
    will not degenerate.
And yet, they dare account themselves
    to be of noble blood.
But fish bred up in dirty pools
    will ever stink of mud.
I promise thee, Menalcas, here,
    I would not them envy
If any spot of gentleness
    in them I might espy.
For if their natures gentle be,
    though birth be never so base,
Of gentlemen (for meet it is)

they ought have name and place.
But when by birth they base are bred
and churlish heart retain,
Though place of gentlemen they have
yet churls they do remain.
A proverb old hath oft been heard,
and now full true is tried:
An ape will ever be an ape
though purple garments hide.
For seldom will the masty course
the hare or else the deer,
But still, according to his kind,
will hold the hog by th'ear.
Unfit are dunghill knights to serve
the town, with spear in field,
Nor strange it seems (a sudden chop)
to leap from whip to shield.
The chiefest man in all our town
that bears the greatest sway
Is Coridon (no kin to me),
a neatherd th'other day.
This Coridon, come from the cart,
in honour chief doth sit
And governs us. Because he hath
a crabbèd, clownish wit,
Now see the churlish cruelty
that in his heart remains.
The seely sheep that shepherds good
have fostered up with pains,
And brought away from stinking dales
on pleasant hills to feed, –
O cruel clownish Coridon!
O cursèd carlish seed! –
The simple sheep constrainèd he
their pasture sweet to leave,
And to their old corrupted grass
enforceth them to cleave.
Such sheep as would not them obey,
but in their pasture bide,
With cruel flames they did consume
and vex on every side.

And with the sheep, the shepherds good
(O hateful hounds of hell)
They did torment, and drive them out
in places far to dwell.
There dièd Daphnes for his sheep,
the chiefest of them all,
And fair Alexis flamed in fire
who never perish shall.
O shepherds, wail for Daphnes' death,
Alexis' hap lament,
And curse the force of cruel hearts
that them to death have sent.
I, since I saw such sinful sights,
did never like the town,
But thought it best to take my sheep
and dwell upon the down.
Whereas I live a pleasant life
and free from cruel hands,
I would not leave the pleasant field
for all the townish lands.
For sith that pride is placèd thus,
and vice set up so high,
And cruelty doth rage so sore,
and men live all awry,
Think'st thou that God will long forbear
his scourge and plague to send
To such as Him do still despise
and never seek to mend?
Let them be sure He will revenge
when they think least upon.
But look, a stormy shower doth rise,
which will fall here anon.
Menalcas, best we now depart;
my cottage us shall keep,
For there is room for thee and me,
and eke for all our sheep.
Some chestnuts have I there in store
with cheese and pleasant whey;
God sends me victuals for my need,
and I sing care away.
Finis Eglogae tertiae.

8 Egloga quarta.
[The Fourth Eclogue.]

Melibeus *Palemon*

O God, that guides the golden globe
where shining shapes do dwell,
O Thou that throwest the thunder thumps
from heavens high, to hell,
What wonders works Thy worthiness?
what marvels dost Thou frame?
What secret sights be subject seen
unto Thy holy name?
A simple shepherd, slain of late
by foolish force of love,
That had not grace such fancies fond
and flames for to remove,
Appearèd late before mine eyes
(alas, I fear to speak)
Not as he here was wont to live
while grief him none did break,
But all in black he clothèd came,
an ugly sight to see,
As they that for their due deserts
with pains tormented be.
My sheep for fear amazèd ran
and fled from hill to dale,
And I alone remainèd there
with countenance wan and pale.
'O Lord,' quoth I, 'what means this thing?
Is this Alexis' sprite?
'Or is it Daphnes' soul that shows
to me this dreadful sight?
'Or comes some fiend of hell abroad,
with fear men to torment?
'Megaera this? or Tisiphon?
or is Alecto sent?
'Whatsoever thou art, that thus dost come,
ghost, hag, or fiend of hell,
'I thee command by Him that lives
thy name and case to tell.'

With this, a stinking smoke I saw
from out his mouth to fly,
And with that same his voice did sound,
'None of them all am I.
'But once thy friend, O Melibei,
Dametas was my name;
'Dametas I, that slew myself,
by force of foolish flame.
'Dametas I, that doting died
in fire of unkind love;
'Dametas I, whom Deiopey
did cause such end to prove.
'The same Dametas here I come,
by licence, unto thee,
'For to declare the woeful state
that happens now to me.
'O Melibei, take heed of love,
of me example take,
'That slew myself, and live in hell,
for Deiopeia's sake.
'I thought that death should me release
from pains and doleful woe,
'But now, alas, the troth is tried
I find it nothing so,
'For look what pain and grief I felt
when I lived here afore,
'With those I now tormented am,
and with ten thousand more.
'I mean not that I burn in love, –
such foolish toys be gone, –
'But griefs in number have I like
and many more upon.
'O cursèd Love, (what should I say?)
that brought me first to pain,
'Well might I once despise thy lore,
but now, alas, in vain.
'With fond affection I did flame
which now I most repent,
'But all too late, alas, I wail,
sith hope of grace is spent.
'The fickle fading form and face

that once so much I sought,
'Hath made me lose the skies above,
and me to hell hath brought.
'Why had I reason dealt to me,
and could not reason use?
'Why gave I bridle to my will
when I might well refuse?
'A wicked will indeed it was
that blinded so my sight,
'That made me on such fading dust
to set my whole delight.
'A fond affection led me then,
when I for God did place
'A creature, cause of all my care,
a fleshy fleeting face,
'A woman, wave of wretchedness,
a pattern pilled of pride,
'A mate of mischief and distress,
for whom, a fool, I died.'
Thus while he spake, I saw, methought,
of hell an ugly fiend,
With loathsome claws, him for to close
and forced him there to end.
And with this same, 'O Melibei,
farewell, farewell,' quoth he,
'Eschew the blaze of fervent flames.
Example take of me.'
My heart with this began to rent,
and all amazed I stood.
'O Lord,' quoth I, 'what flames be these?
What rage, what furies wood
'Doth Love procure to wretched men?
What bondage doth it bring?
'Pain here, and pain in life to come:
O doleful, dreadful thing!'

Palemon I quake to hear this story told,
and, Melibei, I faint,
For sure I thought Dametas had
been placèd like a saint.
I thought that cruel Charon's boat
had missed of him her freight,

And through his death he mounted had
to stars and heavens straight.
How valiantly did he despise
his life in bondage led!
And seeking death with courage high
from love and lady fled.
And is he thus rewarded now?
The ground be cursèd then
That fostered up so fair a face
that lost so good a man
Finis Eglogae quartae.

9 Egloga quinta.
[The Fifth Eclogue.]

Mopsus *Egon*

Some doleful thing there is at hand
thy countenance doth declare:
Thy face, good Egon, void of blood,
thine eyes amazèd stare.
I see thy tears, how they do still
disclose thy secret mind:
Hath Fortune frownèd late on thee?
Hath Cupid been unkind?
Egon A piteous thing to be bewailed,
a desperate act of love, –
O Destinies! such cruel broils
how have you power to move?
Here lived a lady fair of late,
that Claudia men did call,
Of goodly form, – yea such a one
as far surmounted all.
The stately dames that in this Court
to show themselves do lie,
There was not one in all the crew
that could come Claudia nigh.
A worthy knight did love her long,
and for her sake did feel
The pangs of love, that happen still
by frowning Fortune's wheel.

He had a page, Valerius named,
whom so much he did trust,
That all the secrets of his heart
to him declare he must,
And made him all the only means
to sue for his redress,
And to entreat for grace to her
that causèd his distress.
She whenas first she saw his page
was straight with him in love,
That nothing could Valerius' face
from Claudia's mind remove.
By him was Faustus often heard,
by him his suits took place,
By him he often did aspire
to see his lady's face.
This passèd well, till at the length,
Valerius sore did sue,
With many tears beseeching her
his master's grief to rue;
And told her that if she would not
release his master's pain,
He never would attempt her more,
nor see her once again.
She then with mazèd countenance there
and tears that gushing fell,
Astonied answered thus, 'Lo now,
alas, I see too well,
'How long I have deceivèd been
by thee, Valerius, here.
'I never yet believed before
nor till this time did fear
'That thou didst for thy master sue,
but only for my sake
'And for my sight, I ever thought
thou didst thy travail take.
'But now I see the contrary:
thou nothing car'st for me,
'Since first thou knew'st the fiery flames
that I have felt by thee.
'O Lord, how ill thou dost requite

that I for thee have done!
'I curse the time that friendship first
to show I have begun.
'O Lord I Thee beseech, let me
in time revengèd be,
'And let him know that he hath sinned
in this misusing me.
'I cannot think but Fortune once
shall thee reward for all,
'And vengeance due for thy deserts
in time shall on thee fall.
'And tell thy master Faustus now,
if he would have me live,
'That never more he sue to me:
this answer last I give.
'And thou, O traitor vile,
and enemy to my life,
'Absent thyself from out my sight;
procure no greater strife.
'Since that these tears had never force
to move thy stony heart,
'Let never these my wearied eyes
see thee no more. Depart.'
This said, in haste she hieth in,
and there doth vengeance call,
And strake herself with cruel knife
and bloody down doth fall.
This doleful chance when Faustus heard,
lamenting loud he cries,
And tears his hair and doth accuse
the unjust and cruel skies.
And in this raging mood away
he stealeth out alone,
And gone he is no man knows where:
each man for him doth moan.
Valerius, when he doth perceive
his master to be gone,
He weeps and wails in piteous plight
and forth he runs anon.
No man knows where he is become:
some say the woods he took,

Intending there to end his life,
on no man more to look.
The Court laments, the Princess eke
herself doth weep for woe.
Lo, Faustus fled, and Claudia dead,
Valerius vanished so.
Finis Eglogae quintae.

10 Egloga sexta.
[The Sixth Eclogue.]

Felix *Faustus*

Felix O Faustus, whom above the rest
of shepherds here that keep
Upon these holts the number great
of weighty fleecèd sheep
I ever have esteemed, and counted eke
the chiefest friend of all,
What great mishap, what scourge of mind
or grief hath thee befall
That hath thee brought in such a plight
far from thy wonted guise?
What means this countenance all besprent
with tears? – these wretched eyes,
This mourning look, this vesture sad,
this wreath of willow tree?
Unhappy man, why dost thou weep?
What chance hath altered thee?
Tell, tell me soon, I am thy friend;
disclose to me thy grief.
Be not afraid, for friends do serve
to give their friends relief.
Faustus The woeful cause of all my hurt,
good Felix, long ago
Thou knew'st full well; I need not now
by words to double woe.
Since that, alas, all hope is past,
since grief and I am one,
And since the lady of my life
(my fault) I have forgone,

What wouldst thou have me do, O friend?
to joy? in such distress?
Nay, pleasures quite I banish here
and yield to heaviness.
Let griefs torment me evermore,
let never cares away;
Let never Fortune turn her wheel
to give me blissful day.
Love hath me scourged: I am content –
lament not thou my state.
Let spite on me take vengeance now,
let me be torn with hate.
Let her enjoy her happy life,
a flower of golden hue
That closeth when the sun doth set A Marigold
and spreads with Phoebus new.
Sith from my garland now is fall'n
this famous flower sweet,
Let willows wind about my head
(a wreath for wretches meet).

Felix Fie, Faustus, let not fancy fond
in thee bear such a sway.
Expel affections from thy mind
and drive them quite away.
Embrace thine ancient liberty,
let bondage vile be fled:
Let reason rule thy crazèd brain,
place wit in folly's stead.
Since she is gone, what remedy?
Why should'st thou so lament?
Wilt thou destroy thyself with tears
and she to pleasures bent?
Give ear to me, and I will show
the remedies for love
That I have learnèd long ago,
and in my youth did prove;
Such remedies as soon shall quench
the flames of Cupid's fire,
Such remedies as shall delay
the rage of fond desire.
For, Faustus, if thou follow still

the blinded God to please
And wilt not seek by reason's rule
to purchase thine own ease,
Long canst thou not thy friends enjoy,
but bid them all farewell,
And leave thy life, and give thy soul
to deepest floods of hell.
Leave off, therefore, betimes, and let
affection bear no sway,
And now at first the fire quench
before it further stray.
Each thing is easily made to obey
while it is young and green:
The tender twig, that now doth bend,
at length refuseth clean;
The fervent fire, that flaming first
may little water drench,
Whenas it hath obtainèd time
whole rivers cannot quench.
Forsake the town, my Faustus dear,
and dwell upon this plain,
And time shall heal thy festering wound
and absence banish pain.
Above all things fly idleness,
for this doth double strength
To lovers' flames, and makes them rage
till all be lost at length.
Here in these fields are pleasant things
to occupy thy brain:
Behold, how spring revives again,
that winter late had slain;
Behold, the pleasant hills adorned
with divers colours fair;
Give ear to Scylla's lusty songs
rejoicing in the air.
What pleasure canst thou more desire,
than here is for to see?
Thy lusty ewes, with many a lamb,
lo, where they wait on thee.
Think not upon that cursèd face
that makes thee thus her slave,

But well regard the pleasant life
 that here thou seest me have.
When I long time ago did feel
 the flames of Cupid's fire,
These means, lo, then I practisèd
 to cure my fond desire.
I first weighed with myself,
 how fond a thing it seemed
To let my heart lie there in chains
 where I was nought esteemed,
And how with flames I burnt for her,
 that passèd nought for me,
And how these eyes increased my harms
 that first her face did see.
With pensive heart full fraight with thoughts
 I fled from thence away,
And though that Love bade turn my steps
 yet would I never stay,
But from that foul infective air
 where first I took my sore,
I hied in haste, and shunned the place
 to see for evermore.
Each letter that I had received
 from her, I cast away,
And tokens all, I threw them down,
 to my no small dismay.
Then busied I myself in things
 that might me most delight,
And sought the chiefest means I could
 to help my wearied sprite.
Sometime I would behold the fields
 and hills that thou dost see,
Sometime I would betray the birds
 that light on limèd tree:
Especially in shepstare time,
 when thick in flocks they fly,
One would I take, and to her leg
 a limèd line would tie,
And where the flock flew thickest, there
 I would her cast away.
She straight unto the rest would hie

amongst her mates to play,
And pressing in the midst of them
with line and lime and all,
With cleaving wings, entangled fast
they down together fall.
Sometime I would the little fish
with baited hook beguile,
Sometime the crafty fox I would
deceive for all his wile,
Sometime the wolf I would pursue,
sometime the foaming boar,
And when with labour all the day
my wearied limbs were sore,
Then rest and sleep I straightway sought:
no dreams did me affray.
Tormented nought with care, I past
the ling'ring night away.
And thus I clean forgot, in time,
the doting days I saw,
And freed myself, to my great joy,
from yoke of lovers' law.
More of this same I will thee tell
the next time here we meet,
And stronger medicines will I give
to purge that venom sweet.
Behold the day is slipped away,
and stars do fast appear.
Lo, where Calisto, virgin once,
doth shine in skies so clear.
Lo, where old Cepheus walks about,
with twining serpent by.
We will no longer here abide,
but hence will homeward hie.
Finis Eglogae sextae.

11 Egloga septima.
[The Seventh Eclogue.]

Silvanus *Sirenus* *Selvagia*

Sirenus, shepherd good, and thou,

that hast ill luck in love,
The cause of all my hurt by whom
my suits could never prove,
God never let that I should seek
to be revenged of thee,
For when I might have been with ease,
yet would not suffer me
The love that I Diana bare,
on thee to show my spite,
On thee in whom my lady fair
had once her whole delight.
If thy mishaps do not me grieve,
my mischiefs never end.
Think not, Sirenus, that because
Diana was thy friend,
I bear thee worser will; assure thyself
so base my love never seemed
That only I should favour her,
but all that she esteemed.

Sirenus Thou either art, Silvanus, born
example for to give
To us that know not how
when Fortune frowns to live,
Or else hath Nature placed in thee
so strong and stout a mind,
Sufficing not, thine ills alone
to bear, but means to find
That may the griefs of others help.
I see thou art so bent
That Fortune can thee not amaze,
for all her mischiefs meant.
I promise thee, Silvanus, here,
time plain in thee doth show,
How daily she discovers things
that erst did men not know.
I cannot bear the griefs I feel,
my force is all too faint,
I never could, as thou canst, stint
the tears of my complaint.
Diana hath procured the pains
that I shall never end;

When first she falsed her troth to me,
she killed a faithful friend.

Silvanus I marvel how she could so soon
put thee out of her mind.
I well remember since thou went'st
alone I did her find
In place that sorrow seemed to shape,
where no man stood her nigh,
But only I (unhappy wretch)
that heard her woeful cry.
And this with tears aloud she said,
'O wretch in ill time born,
'What chance hast thou, that thus thou hast
Sirenus sweet forlorn?
'Give over pleasures now,
let never joy thee please,
'Seek all the cruel means thou canst
that may thy heart disease.
'When thou dost him forget I wish
all mischiefs on thee light,
'And after death, the fiends of hell
torment thy living sprite.'

Sirenus What man would here believe
that she that thus could speak,
In so short time as I have been
away, would promise break?
O steadfastness and constancy,
how seldom are you found
In women's hearts to have your seats,
or long abiding ground?
Who look how much more earnest they
at first their hearts do set,
So much more sooner evermore,
where late they loved, forget.
Full well could ever I believe
all women guilty of this,
Save her alone, in whom I judge
never nature wrought amiss.
But since her marriage how she speeds
Silvan I pray thee tell?

Silvanus Some say she likes it very ill,

and I believe it well;
For Delius, he that hath her now,
although he wealthy be,
Is but a lout, and hath in him
no handsome quality.
For as for all such things wherein
we shepherds have delight,
As in quoiting, leaping, singing or
to sound a bagpipe right,
In all these things he is but an ass,
and nothing do he can.
They say 'tis qualities, but tush,
it's riches makes a man.

Sirenus What woman is that that cometh here,
Silvanus, canst thou tell?

Silvanus It's one hath sped as well in love
as we: I know her well.
She is one of fair Diana's friends,
who keeps her beasts below
Not far from hence; by her thou maist
Diana's state well know.
She lovèd here a shepherd, called
Alanius, long ago,
Who favours one Ismenia now,
the cause of all her woe.

Selvagia No place so fit for thee as this:
lo, here Silvanus stands,
Who hath received like luck to thine
at cruel Fortune's hands;
This company beseems thee well.
Fair shepherds both, good-den.

Silvanus To thee Selvagia eke, of hope
whom Love hath spoilèd clean,
A thousand better days I wish
than thou hast had before.

Selvagia At length may better fortune fall,
for worse cannot be more.
To trust the feignèd words of men,
lo, thus poor women speeds.

Silvanus And men do smart not through your words,
but your unconstant deeds.

For you when earnestliest you love,
    nothing can chance so light,
But if a toy come in your brain,
    your mind is altered quite.
If we but once absent ourselves
    the shortest time we may,
So much unconstant is your minds
    love soareth straight away.
Example take Sirenus here,
    whom once Diana loved,
As all we know, and look how soon
    her mind is now removed.
No, no, there is not one of you
    that constant can remain.

Selvagia You judge but of malicious heart,
    and of a jealous brain.
All things you do yourselves esteem,
    and men must bear no blame.
Of your dissembling noughty deeds
    we women bear the shame.

Sirenus Fair damsel, if you can perceive,
    Silvanus true doth say:
There is not one amongst you all
    but doth from reason stray.
What is the cause that women thus
    in their unconstancy,
Do cast a man from highest hap
    to deepest misery?
It's nothing else, I you assure,
    but that you know not well
What thing is love, and what you have
    in hand you cannot tell.
Your simple wits are all too weak
    unfeignèd love to know,
And thereof doth forgetfulness
    in you so shortly grow.

Selvagia Sirenus, judge not so of us;
    our wits be not so base,
But that we know as well as you
    what's what in every case;
And women eke, there are enow

that could if they were brought
Teach men to live, and more to love,
if love might well be taught.
And for all this, yet do I think
nothing can worser be
Than women's state: it is the worst,
I think, of each degree.
For if they show but gentle words
you think for love they die;
And if they speak not when you list
then straight you say, they are high,
And that they are disdainful dames;
and if they chance to talk,
Then count you them for chattering pies
whose tongues must always walk;
And if perhaps they do forbear,
and silence chance to keep,
Then tush, she is not for company,
she is but a simple sheep;
And if they bear good will to one
then straight they are judgèd nought,
And if ill name to shun they leave
unconstant they are thought.
Who now can please these jealous heads?
The fault is all in you,
For women never would change their minds
if men would still be true.

Sirenus Lo, this I well could answer you,
but time doth bid me stay.
And women must the last word have,
no man may say them nay.
Pass over this, and let us hear
what luck you have had in love,
And show if ever love of man
your constant heart could move.
No fitter place can be than this,
here may you safely rest,
Thus sitting here, declare at large
the secrets of your breast.

Selvagia Nay, longer here we may not bide,
but home we must away.

Lo, how the sun denies his beams,
depriving us of day.
Finis Eglogae septimae.

12 Egloga octava.
[The Eighth Eclogue.]

Coridon *Cornix*

Now rageth Titan fierce above,
his beams on earth do beat,
Whose hot reflection makes us feel
an over-fervent heat.
With fiery Dog he forward flames,
hot agues up he drives,
And sends them down, with boiling blood,
to shorten misers' lives.
Lo how the beasts lies under trees,
how all thing seeks the shade!
O blessèd God, that some defence
for every hurt hast made,
Behold this pleasant broadleaved beech
and springing fountain clear,
Here shade enough, here water cold,
come, Cornix, rest we here,
And let us songs begin to sing;
our purse and hearts be light,
We fear not we, the tumbling world,
we break no sleeps by night.

Cornix Both place and time, my Coridon,
exhorteth me to sing,
Not of the wretched lovers' lives,
but of the immortal king,
Who gives us pasture for our beasts
and blesseth our increase;
By whom, while other cark and toil,
we live at home with ease;
Who keeps us down, from climbing high
where honour breeds debate,
And here hath granted us to live
in simple shepherd's state:

A life that sure doth far exceed
each other kind of life.
O happy state, that doth content,
how far be we from strife?
Of Him, therefore, me list to sing,
and of no wanton toys,
For Him to love, and Him to praise,
surmounts all other joys.
O shepherds, leave Cupido's camp,
the end whereof is vile;
Remove Dame Venus from your eyes
and harken here a while.
A God there is, that guides the globe,
and framed the fickle sphere,
And placèd hath the stars above
that we do gaze on here,
By whom we live, (unthankful beasts)
by whom we have our health,
By whom we gain our happy states,
by whom we get our wealth.
A God, that sends us what we need,
a God, that us defends,
A God, from whom the angels high
on mortal man attends,
A God, of such a clemency,
that whoso Him doth love
Shall here be sure to rest a while,
and always rest above.
But we for Him do little care,
His hests we nought esteem,
But hunt for things that He doth hate:
most pleasant those do seem.
Unthankful misers! what do we?
What mean we thus to stray
From such a God, so merciful,
to walk a worser way?
May nought His benefits procure?
May nought His mercies move?
May nothing bind, but needs we must
give hate to Him for love?
O happy (ten times) is the man,

(a bird full rare to find)
That loveth God with all his heart
and keeps His laws in mind.
He shall be blest in all his works,
and safe in every time,
He shall sweet quietness enjoy,
while other smart for crime.
The threatening chances of the world
shall never him annoy;
When Fortune frowns on foolish men
he shall be sure to joy.
For why? the angels of the Lord
shall him defend always,
And set him free, at every harms
and hurts at all assays.
Even He that kept the Prophet safe Daniel
from mouths of lions wild,
And He that once preserved in flags Moses
the seely sucking child,
The God that fed, by raven's bill, Elias
the teacher of His word,
Shall him (no doubt) in safety keep
from famine, fire, and sword.
Not he, whom poets old have feigned
to live in heaven high, Jupiter
Embracing boys (O filthy thing)
in beastly lechery;
Nor Juno, she (that wrinkled jade) Juno
that queen of skies is called;
Nor sullen Saturn, churlish chuff, Saturn
with scalp of canker bald;
Nor fuming fool, with fiery face, Mars
that moves the fighter's mind;
Nor Venus, she (that wanton wench) Venus
that guides the shooter blind, Cupido
Can thee defend, as God will do,
for they were sinful fools,
Whom first the blind high-witted Greek Homerus
brought into wise men's schools.
No, none of these, but God alone,
ought worship for to have,

For they, for all their honour once,
rest yet in stinking grave.
Here hast thou heard the happy state
of them that live in fear
Of God, and love Him best: now list,
His foes' reward to hear,
And first know thou that every man
that from this God doth go,
And follow lust, him He accounts
to be His deadly foe.
This mighty King of whom we talk,
as He is merciful,
And suffers long, revenging slow,
so when we be thus dull
That we will not perceive in time
the goodness of His grace,
His favour straight He doth withdraw
and turns away His face,
And to Himself then doth He say,
'How long shall I permit
'These stubborn beasts for to rebel?
and shall I love them yet,
'That hate Me thus? or have I need
their loving minds to crave?
'I ask no more but only love,
and that I cannot have.
'Well, well, I will not care for them
that thus do Me despise;
'Let them go live even as they list,
I turn away Mine eyes.'
When God hath thus said to Himself,
then doth the brainless fool
Cast bridle off, and out he runs,
neglecting virtue's school.
Then doth the devil give him line
and let him run at large,
And pleasure makes his mariner,
to row in vice's barge.
Then up the sails of wilfulness
he hoises high in haste,
And fond affection blows him forth,

a wind that Pluto placed.
Then cuts he swift the seas of sin,
and through the channel deep,
With joyful mind, he fleets apace,
whom pleasure brings asleep.
Then who so happy thinks himself?
Who dreams of joy but he?
'Tush, tush,' saith he, 'to think of God,
in age sufficeth me;
'Now will I pass my pleasant youth,
such toys becomes this age,
'And God shall follow me,' saith he,
'I will not be His page.
'I will be proud, and look aloft;
I will my body deck
'With costly clothes above my state:
who then dare give me check?'
Coridon Garments sometime so guard a knave
that he dare mate a knight,
Yet have I seen a *Nec* in hemp
for checking often light.
Cornix 'The Peacock's plume shall not me pass
that nature finely framed,
'For coloured silks shall set me forth,
that nature shall be shamed.
'My sword shall get me valiant fame,
I will be Mars outright,
'And Mars, you know, must Venus have,
To recreate his sprite.
'I will oppress the simple knave, –
shall slaves be saucy now?
'Nay, I will teach the needy dogs
with cap to crouch and bow.'
Thus fareth he, and thus he lives,
no whit esteeming God,
In health, in joy, and lustiness,
free from the smarting rod;
But in the midst of all his mirth,
while he suspecteth least,
His happy chance begins to change
and eke his fleeting feast.

For death (that old devouring wolf)
whom goodmen nothing fear,
Comes sailing fast in galley black
and when he spies him near
Doth board him straight, and grapples fast,
and then begins the fight.
In riot leaps, as captain chief,
and from the mainmast right
He downward comes, and surfeit, then,
assaileth by and by,
Then vile diseases forward shoves,
with pains and grief thereby.
Life stands aloft, and fighteth hard,
but pleasure all aghast
Doth leave his oar, and out he flies;
then death approacheth fast,
And gives the charge so sore, that needs
must life begin to fly.
Then farewell all. The wretched man
with carrion corpse doth lie,
Whom Death himself flings overboard
amid the seas of sin:
The place where late he sweetly swam,
now lies he drownèd in.
Continual torment him awaits,
(a monster vile to tell)
That was begot of due desert,
and reigneth now in hell;
With greedy mouth he always feeds
upon the sin-drowned soul,
Whose greedy paws do never cease
in sinful floods to prowl.
Lo! This the end of every such
as here lives lustily,
Neglecting God: thou seest, in vice
do live, in sin do die.
What should I speak of all their harms
that happens them in life?
Their conscience pricked, their barren blood,
their toil, their grief, their strife,
With mischiefs heapèd many a one,

which they do never try
That love and fear the mighty God
that rules and reigns on high.
Too long it were to make discourse,
and Phoebus down descends,
And in the clouds his beams doth hide
which tempest sure portends.
Look how the beasts begin to fling
and cast their heads on high,
The heronshew mounts above the clouds,
the crows each where do cry;
All this shows rain: time bids us go;
come Coridon, away,
Take up thy staff, fetch in thy beasts,
let us go while we may,

Coridon Cornix, agreed, go thou before;
yon cursèd bull of mine
I must go drive: he never bides
among my father's kine.

Finis Eglogae octavae.

EPITAPHS

13 An Epitaph of
the Lord Sheffield's death.

When brutish broil and rage of war
in clownish hearts began,
When tigers stout in tanner's bond
unmuzzled all they ran,
The noble Sheffield, Lord by birth
and of a courage good,
By clubbish hands of crabbèd clowns
there spent his noble blood.
His noble birth availèd not,
his honour all was vain,
Amid the press of masty curs
the valiant Lord was slain;
And after such a sort (O ruth!)
that who can tears suppress?
To think that dunghill dogs should daunt
the flower of worthiness.
Whileas the ravening wolves he prayed
his guiltless life to save,
A bloody butcher big and blunt,
a vile unwieldy knave,
With beastly blow of boisterous bill
at him (O Lord) let drive,
And cleft his head, and said therewith
'Shalt thou be left alive?'
O Lord, that I had present been,
and Hector's force withal,
Before that from his carlish hands

the cruel bill did fall.
Then should that peasant vile have felt
the clap upon his crown
That should have dazed his doggèd heart
from driving Lords adown;
Then should my hands have saved thy life,
good Lord whom dear I loved;
Then should my heart in doubtful case
full well to thee been proved.
But all in vain thy death I wail,
thy corpse in earth doth lie.
Thy king and country for to serve
thou didst not fear to die.
Farewell, good Lord, thy death bewail
all such as well thee knew,
And every man laments thy case,
and Googe thy death doth rue.

14 An Epitaph of M. Shelley slain at Musselburgh.

When Mars had movèd mortal hate
and forcèd fumish heat,
And high Bellona had decreed
to sit with sword in seat,
The Scots untrue, with fighting hand
their promise to deny,
Assembled fast, and England thought
the troth with them to try;
Chose Musselburgh their fighting place,
amid those barren fields
Their breach of faith there not to try
with troth, but trothless shields.
In battle brave and army strong
encampèd sure they lay,
Ten Scots to one (a dreadful thing,
a doleful fighting day)
That Englishmen were all aghast,
with quaking staves in hand,
To see their enemies lie so near,
and death with them to stand.
No other remedy there was

but fight it out or fly,
And who should first the onset give
was sure therein to die.
Thus all dismayed and wrapped in fear
with doubtful mind they stand,
If best it be, with fight of foot
to strive, or flight of hand.
Till at the length, a captain stout
with haughty mind gan speak:
'O cowards all, and maidly men,
of courage faint and weak,
'Unworthy come of Brutus' race!
is this your manhood gone,
'And is there none, you dastards all,
that dare them set upon?'
Then Shelley all inflamed with heat,
with heat of valiant mind:
'No cowards we, nor maidly men,
ne yet of dastards' kind
'I would you wist did ever come,
but dare be bold to try
'Our manhood here, though nought appear
but death to all men's eye.'
And with these words (O noble heart)
no longer there he stayed,
But forth before them all he sprang
as one no whit dismayed.
With chargèd staff on foaming horse
his spurs with heels he strikes,
And forward runs with swifty race
among the mortal pikes.
And in this race with famous end,
to do his country good,
Gave onset first upon his foes,
and lost his vital blood.
Finis.

15 An Epitaph of Master Thomas Phaer.

The haughty verse that Maro wrote
made Rome to wonder much;
And marvel none: for why? the style
and weightiness was such,
That all men judged Parnassus Mount
had cleft herself in twain,
And brought forth one that seemed to drop
from out Minerva's brain.
But wonder more may Britain great,
where Phaer did flourish late,
And barren tongue with sweet accord
reduced to such estate
That Virgil's verse hath greater grace
in foreign foot obtained
Than in his own, who whilst he lived
each other poets stained.
The noble Henry Howard once
that raught eternal fame,
With mighty style, did bring a piece
of Virgil's work in frame,
And Grimald gave the like attempt,
and Douglas won the ball,
Whose famous wit in Scottish rhyme
had made an end of all.
But all these same did Phaer excel,
I dare presume to write,
As much as doth Apollo's beams
the dimmest star in light.
The envious Fates (O pity great)
had great disdain to see
That us amongst there should remain
so fine a wit as he,
And in the midst of all his toil
did force him hence to wend,
And leave a work unperfect so,
that never man shall end.

16 An Epitaph of
the Death of Nicholas Grimald.

Behold this fleeting world how all things fade,
How everything doth pass and wear away,
Each state of life, by common course and trade,
Abides no time, but hath a passing day.
For look as life, that pleasant dame, hath brought
The pleasant years and days of lustiness,
So death our foe consumeth all to nought,
Envying these, with dart doth us oppress,
And that which is the greatest grief of all,
The greedy gripe doth no estate respect,
But where he comes he makes them down to fall;
Ne stays he at the high sharp-witted sect,
For if that wit, or worthy eloquence,
Or learning deep, could move him to forbear,
O Grimald, then thou hadst not yet gone hence,
But here hadst seen full many an agèd year,
Ne had the Muses lost so fine a flower,
Nor had Minerva wept to leave thee so.
If wisdom might have fled the fatal hour,
Thou hadst not yet been suffered for to go.
A thousand doltish geese we might have spared,
A thousand witless heads death might have found,
And taken them, for whom no man had cared,
And laid them low in deep oblivious ground.
But Fortune favours fools, as old men say,
And lets them live, and takes the wise away.
Finis.

SONNETS

17 To Master Alexander Nowell.

The Muses joy, and well they may to see
So well their labour come to good success
That they sustainèd long ago in thee.
Minerva smiles, Phoebus can do no less,
But over all, they chiefly do rejoice
That leaving things which are but fond and vain,
Thou diddest choose (O good and happy choice)
In sacred schools thy lucky years to train,
By which thou hast obtained (O happy thing)
To learn to live while other wander wide,
And by thy life to please the immortal king,
Than which so good, nothing can be applied.
Law gives the gain, and Physic fills the purse,
Promotions high, gives Arts to many one,
But this is it, by which we scape the curse
And have the bliss of God, when we be gone.
Is this but only Scriptures for to read?
No, no! Not talk, but life gives this in deed.

18 To Doctor Bale.

Good agèd Bale, that with thy hoary hairs
Dost yet persist to turn the painful book,
O happy man, that hast obtained such years,
And leav'st not yet on papers pale to look!
Give over now to beat thy wearied brain,
And rest thy pen that long hath laboured sore.
For agèd men unfit, sure, is such pain,

And thee beseems to labour now no more.
But thou I think Don Plato's part will play,
With book in hand to have thy dying day.
Finis.

19 To M. Edward Cobham.

Old Socrates, whose wisdom did excel,
And passed the reach of wisest in his time,
Surmounted all that on the earth did dwell,
That craggy hills of virtue high did climb;
That Socrates, my Cobham, did allow
Each man in youth himself in glass to view,
And willed them oft to use the same: but how?
Not to delight in form of fading hue,
Nor to be proud thereof, as many be,
But for to strive by beauty of the mind
For to adorn the beauty he doth see.
If warlike form Dame Nature him assigned,
By virtuous life then countenance for to get,
That shall deface the fairest of them all,
Such beauty as no age nor years will fret,
That flies with fame, when fickle form doth fail.
Thus much I say, that here to thee present
My words, a glass for thee to look upon,
To thee whom God in tender years hath lent
A towardness that may be mused upon,
Such towardness as in more graver years
Doth sure a hope of greater things pretend;
Thy noble mind, that to thy friends appears,
Doth show the blood whereof thou dost descend;
The gentleness thou usest unto all such
As smally have deserved good will of thee,
Doth show the grace thou hast, which sure is much,
As ever yet in any I did see;
Thy wit as ripe as Nature well can give
Declares a greater hope than all the rest:
That shall remain to thee whilst thou dost live,
In desperate ills a medicine ever prest.
The good behaviour of thyself in place
Wheresoever that thou chancest for to light,

So much both beauty, mind, and wit doth grace
As well can be required of any wight.
What resteth now? but only God to praise,
Of whom thou hast received these gifts of thine.
So shalt thou long live here with happy days,
And after death, the starry skies shalt climb.
Let noughty men say what they list to thee;
Trade thou thyself in serving Him above:
No sweeter service can devisèd be.
Whom if thou fear'st and faithfully dost love,
Be sure nothing on earth shall thee annoy,
Be sure He will thee from each harm defend,
Be sure thou shalt long time thy life enjoy,
And after many years to have a blessèd end.
Finis.

20 Of Edwards of the Chapel.

Divine Camenes, that with your sacred food
Have fed and fostered up from tender years
A happy man that in your favour stood,
Edwards, in Court that cannot find his feres,
Your names be blest, that in this present age
So fine a head by art have framèd out,
Whom some hereafter, helped by poet's rage,
Perchance may match, but none shall pass (no doubt).
O Plautus, if thou wert alive again,
That comedies so finely didst indite,
Or Terence, thou that with thy pleasant brain
The hearer's mind on stage didst much delight,
What would you say, sirs, if you should behold
As I have done, the doings of this man?
No word at all, to swear I durst be bold,
But burn with tears that which with mirth began,
I mean your books, by which you gat your name,
To be forgot, you would commit to flame.
Alas, I would, Edwards, more tell thy praise,
But at thy name my muse amazèd stays.

21 To L. Blundeston.

Some men be counted wise that well can talk,

And some because they can each man beguile,
Some for because they know well cheese from chalk,
And can be sure, weep whoso list, to smile.
But, Blund'ston, him I call the wisest wight,
Whom God gives grace to rule affections right.

***21a** The Answer of L. Blundeston to the same.

Affections seeks high honour's frail estate,
Affections doth the golden mean reprove,
Affections turns the friendly heart to hate,
Affections breed without discretion love;
Both wise and happy, Googe, he may be hight,
Whom God gives grace to rule affections right.

22 To Alexander Neville.

The little fish, that in the stream doth fleet
With broad forth-stretchèd fins for his disport,
Whenas he spies the fish's bait so sweet,
In haste he hies, fearing to come too short,
But all too soon (alas) his greedy mind,
By rash attempt, doth bring him to his bane;
For where he thought a great relief to find,
By hidden hook, the simple fool is ta'en.
So fareth man, that wanders here and there,
Thinking no hurt to happen him thereby,
He runs amain to gaze on beauty's cheer,
Takes all for gold that glisters in the eye,
And never leaves to feed by looking long
On beauty's bait, where bondage lies enwrapped:
Bondage that makes him sing another song,
And makes him curse the bait that him entrapped.
Neville, to thee, that lovest their wanton looks,
Feed on the bait, but yet beware the hooks.

***22a** Alexander Neville's Answer to the same.

It is not cursèd Cupid's dart,
    nor Venus' cankered spite,
It is not vengeance of the gods

that wretched hearts doth smite
With restless rage of careful love:
no, no, thy force alone,
Affection fond, doth stir these flames.
Thou causest us to moan
And wail, and curse our wretched states.
Our thrice unhappy plights,
Our sighs, and powdered sobs with tears,
our grievous groaning sprites,
Thy hateful malice doth procure,
O fancy, flaming fiend
Of hell. For thou in outward shape
and colour of a friend,
Dost by thy snares and slimèd hooks
entrap the wounded hearts,
From whence these hell-like torments spring,
and ever-grieving smarts.
Whence gripe of mind, with changèd cheer,
whence face besmeared with tears,
Whence thousand mischiefs more, wherewith
such misers' lives outwears.
Our gazing eyes on beauty's bait
do work our endless bane;
Our eyes, I say, do work our woe,
our eyes procure our pain.
These are the traps to vexèd minds,
here gins and snares do lie,
Here fire and flames by fancy framed
in breast do broil and fry.
O Googe, the bait soon spièd is,
soon viewed their wanton looks,
Whereon to feed, and yet to shun
the privy lurking hooks,
There pain, there toil, there labour is,
there, there lies endless strife.
O happy, then, that man account,
whose well directed life
Can fly those ills which fancy stirs,
and live from bondage free:
A Phoenix right on th'earth (no doubt),
a bird full rare to see.

23 To M. Henry Cobham
of the most blessed state of Life.

The happiest life that here we have,
My Cobham, if I shall define,
The goodliest state twixt birth and grave,
Most gracious days and sweetest time,
The fairest face of fading life,
Race rightliest run in ruthful ways,
The safest means to shun all strife,
The surest staff in fickle days,
I take not, I, as some do take,
To gape and gawn for honours high,
But Court and Caiser to forsake,
And live at home full quietly.
I well do mind what he once said,
Who bade, Court not in any case,
For virtue is in Courts decayed,
And vice with states hath chiefest place.
Not Court but Country, I do judge,
Is it where lies the happiest life;
In Country grows no grating grudge,
In Country stands not sturdy strife,
In Country Bacchus hath no place,
In Country Venus hath defect,
In Country Thraso hath no grace,
In Country few of Gnatho's sect,
But these same four and many moe
In Court thou shalt be sure to find.
For they have vowed not thence to go,
Because in Court dwells idle mind.
In Country maist thou safely rest
And fly all these, if that thou list.
The Country, therefore, judge I best,
Where godly life doth vice resist,
Where virtuous exercise with joy
Doth spend the years that are to run,
Where vices few may thee annoy:
This life is best when all is done.

24 To Alexander Neville

of the blessed State of him
that feels not the force of Cupid's flames.

As oft as I remember with myself
The fancies fond that flame by foolish love,
And mark the Furies fell, the blinded elf
And Venus, she that reigns so sore above,
As oft as I do see the woeful state
Of lovers all, and eke their misery,
The one's desiring mind, the other's hate,
Troth with the one, with the other treachery,
So oft say I, that blessèd is the wight,
Yea, Neville, blessed, and double blessed again,
That can by reason rule his mind aright,
And take such foolish fading toys for vain.

***24a** Alexander Neville's Answer to the same.

The plungèd mind in floods of griefs,
the senses drownèd quite,
The heart oppressed, the flesh consumed,
the changèd state outright,
The body dried by broiling blaze
of privy scorching flame,
The doleful face, the countenance sad,
the drooping courage tame,
The scalding sighs, the grievous groans,
the burning rage of fire,
The earnest suit, the fruitless toil,
the deep and hot desire,
The brains quite bruised and crushed with cares,
the ever-during sore,
The very pains of hell itself,
with thousand mischiefs more,
Which wounded hearts enflamed with love
with grief do overflow,
And works their endless plague and spite
till death from thence do grow:
All these conclude him blessed (my Googe)
and treble blessed again,
That taught by tract of time can take
such fading toys for vain.

25 To Mistress A.

Since I so long have lived in pain
and burnt for love of thee,
(O cruel heart) dost thou no more
esteem the love of me?
Regard'st thou not the health of him
that thee, above the rest
Of creatures all, and next to God,
hath dearest in his breast?
Is pity placed from thee so far?
is gentleness exiled?
Hast thou been fostered in the caves
of wolves or lions wild?
Hast thou been so? why then, no force,
the less I marvel, I,
Such as the dam, such is the young,
experience true doth try.
Sith thou art of so fierce a mind,
why did not God then place
In thee, with such a tiger's heart,
a foul ill-favoured face?
Sure for no other end, but that
He likes no lover's trade,
And thee therefore, a raging fiend,
an angel's face hath made.
Such one as thou was Gorgon once,
as ancient poets tell,
Who with her beauty mazèd men,
and now doth reign in hell.
But mercy yet of thee I crave,
if ought in thee remain,
And let me not so long the force
of flaming fire sustain.
Let pity joined with beauty be,
so shall I not disdain
My blood, my heart, my life to spend
with toil, with strife, and pain,
To do thee good, my breath to lose,
if need shall so require;
But for my service and my pains

thou givest me hate for hire.
Well now take this for end of all,
I love and thou dost hate,
Thou livest in pleasures happily,
and I in wretched state.
Pains cannot last for evermore,
but time and end will try,
And time shall tell me in my age,
how youth led me awry.
Thy face that me tormented so,
in time shall sure decay,
And all that I do like or love
shall vanish quite away.
Thy face in time shall wrinkled be,
at which I shall be glad,
To see thy form transformèd thus,
that made me once so sad.
Then shall I blame my folly much,
and thank the mightiest king,
That hath me saved till such a day
to see so fond a thing.
And till that time I will keep close
my flames and let them blaze
All secretly within my breast:
no man on me shall gaze.
I will not trespass sinfully,
for God shall give me grace
To see the time wherein I shall
neglect thy foolish face.
And till that time, adieu to thee,
God keep thee far from me,
And send thee in that place to dwell,
that I shall never see.

26 To George Holmedon of a running Head.

The greatest vice that happens unto men,
And yet a vice that many common have,
As ancient writers weigh with sober pen,
Who gave their doom by force of wisdom grave,
The sorest maim, the greatest evil sure,

The vilest plague that students can sustain,
And that which most doth ignorance procure,
My Holmeden, is to have a running brain.
For who is he that leads more restless life,
Or who can ever live more ill bestead?
In fine, who lives in greater care and strife
Than he that hath such an unsteadfast head?
But what is this? methinks I hear thee say,
'Physician, take thine own disease away.'

27 To the Translation of Palingen.

The labour sweet that I sustained in thee,
O Palingen, when I took pen in hand,
Doth grieve me now, as oft as I thee see
But half hewed out, before mine eyes to stand;
For I must needs (no help) a while go toil
In studies that no kind of muse delight,
And put my plough in gross untillèd soil,
And labour thus with overwearied sprite;
But if that God do grant me greater years
And take me not from hence before my time,
The Muses nine, the pleasant singing feres,
Shall so enflame my mind with lust to rhyme
That Palingen, I will not leave thee so,
But finish thee according to my mind.
And if it be my chance away to go,
Let some thee end, that here remain behind.

28 The Heart absent.

Sweet muse, tell me, where is my heart become?
For well I feel it is from hence away.
My senses all doth sorrow so benumb,
That absent thus, I cannot live a day.
I know for troth, there is a special place
Whereas it most desireth for to be,
For oft it leaves me thus in doleful case,
And hither comes at length again to me.
Would'st thou so fain be told where is thy heart?
Sir Fool, in place whereas it should not be,

Tied up so fast that it can never start
Till wisdom get again thy liberty;
In place where thou as safe mayst dwell, sweet daw,
As may the hart lie by the lion's paw,
And where for thee as much be sure they pass,
As did the master once for Aesop's ass.

29 To Alexander Neville.

If thou canst banish idleness
    Cupido's bow is broke, Ovid
And well thou mayest despise his brands
    clean void of flame and smoke.
What moved the king Aegisthus once
    to love with vile excess?
The cause at hand doth straight appear:
    he lived in idleness.
Finis.

***29a** The Answer of A. Neville to the same.

The lack of labour maims the mind,
And wit and reason quite exiles,
And reason fled, flames fancy blind,
And fancy she forthwith beguiles
The senseless wight, that swiftly sails
Through deepest floods of vile excess.
Thus vice abounds, thus virtue quails,
By means of drowsy idleness.

30 To Mistress D.

Not from the high Cytherian hill
    nor from that lady's throne
From whence flies forth the wingèd boy
    that makes some sore to groan,
But nearer hence this token comes,
    from out the Dungeon deep,
Where never Pluto yet did reign
    nor Proserpine did sleep,
Whereas thy faithful servant lives,

whom duty moves aright,
To wail that he so long doth lack
his own dear mistress' sight.

31 Out of an old Poet.

Fie, fie, I loath to speak: wilt thou, my lust,
Compel me now to do so foul an act?
Nay, rather God with flame consume to dust
My carrion vile, than I perform this fact.
Let rather thoughts that long have wearied me,
Or sickness such as fancy fond hath brought,
O gaping hell, drive me now down to thee,
Let boiling signs consume me all to nought.

32

Once musing as I sat,
and candle burning by,
When all were hushed, I might discern
a simple seely fly,
That flew before mine eyes
with free rejoicing heart,
And here and there with wings did play
as void of pain and smart.
Sometime by me she sat
when she had played her fill,
And ever when she rested had
about she flittered still.
When I perceived her well,
rejoicing in her place,
'O happy fly,' quoth I, and eke
'O worm in happy case!
'Which two of us is best?
I that have reason? no:
'But thou that reason art without
and therewith void of woe.
'I live and so dost thou,
but I live all in pain,
'And subject am to her, alas,
that makes my grief her gain.

'Thou livest, but feel'st no grief;
no love doth thee torment.
'A happy thing for me it were,
if God were so content,
'That thou with pen wert placèd here
and I sat in thy place;
'Then I should joy as thou dost now
and thou should'st wail thy case.'

33

When I do hear thy name,
alas, my heart doth rise,
And seeks forthwith to see the salve
that most contents mine eyes.
But when I see thy face,
that hath procured my pain,
Then boils my blood in every part
and beats in every vein.
Thy voice when I do hear,
then colour comes and goes;
Sometime as pale as earth I look,
sometime as red as rose.
If thy sweet face do smile,
then who so well as I?
If thou but cast a scornful look,
then out alas! I die.
But still I live in pain,
my fortune willeth so
That I should burn, and thou yet know
no whit of all my woe.

34

Unhappy tongue, why didst thou not consent
When first mine eyes did view that princely face
To show goodwill, that heart oppressed then meant,
And whilst time was, to sue for present grace?
O fainting heart, why didst thou then conceal
Thine inward fires, that flamed in every vein?
When pity and gentleness were bent to heal,
Why didst thou not declare thy raging pain?

When well thou might'st have moved her gentle mind,
Why didst thou then keep back thy woeful plaints?
Thou knew'st full well, redress is hard to find,
When in thy own affairs, thy courage faints.
But since she is gone, bewail thy grief no more,
Since thou thyself wert causer of the sore.

35 Oculi augent dolorem.
Out of sight, out of mind.

The oftener seen, the more I lust,
The more I lust, the more I smart,
The more I smart, the more I trust,
The more I trust, the heavier heart,
The heavy heart breeds mine unrest,
Thy absence, therefore, like I best.

The rarer seen, the less in mind,
The less in mind, the lesser pain,
The lesser pain, less grief I find,
The lesser grief, the greater gain,
The greater gain, the merrier I,
Therefore I wish thy sight to fly.

The further off, the more I joy,
The more I joy, the happier life,
The happier life, less hurts annoy,
The lesser hurts, pleasure most rife,
Such pleasures rife shall I obtain
When distance doth depart us twain.
Finis.

36

Accuse not God, if fancy fond
do move thy foolish brain
To wail for love, for thou thyself
art cause of all thy pain.
Finis.

37

Two lines shall tell the grief
    that I by love sustain:
I burn, I flame, I faint, I freeze,
    of hell I feel the pain.

38 Of the unfortunate choice
of his Valentine.

The pains that all the Furies fell
    can cast from Limbo lake,
Each torment of those hellish brains
    where crawleth many a snake,
Each mischief that therein doth lie,
    each smart that may be found,
Fly from those fiendish claws a while,
    with flames break up the ground,
Light here upon this cursèd hand,
    make here your dwelling place,
And plague the part that durst presume
    his master to disgrace;
Which thrust amongst a number of
    so many princely names,
And where thy mistress had her place
    amongst the chiefest dames,
Durst thus presume to leave her there
    and draw a stranger wight,
And by thine own unhappy draught
    torment my pallèd sprite.

39 The uncertainty of Life.

No vainer thing there can be found
    amid this vale of strife,
As ancient men report have made,
    than trust uncertain life.
This true we daily find,
    by proofs of many years,
And many times the troth is tried
    by loss of friendly feres.
Hope whoso list in life
    hath but uncertain stay,

As tail of eel that harder held
doth sooner slide away.
When least we think thereof,
most near approacheth it,
And suddenly possess the place
where life before did sit.
How many have been seen
in health to go to rest,
And yet ere morningtide have been
with cruel death oppressed.
How many in their meals
have joyfully been set,
That suddenly in all their feast
hath yielded earth their debt.
Sith thus the life is nought
that in this world we trust,
And that for all the pomp and pride,
the body turns to dust,
Hope for the life above,
which far surmounteth all;
With virtuous mind await the time
when God for us doth call.

40 A Refusal.

Sith Fortune favours not,
and all things backward go,
And sith your mind hath so decreed,
to make an end of woe,
Sith now is no redress,
but hence I must away,
Farewell, I waste no vainer words,
I hope for better day.

41 Of Mistress D.S.

Thy filèd words that from thy mouth did flow,
Thy modest look, with gesture of Diane,
Thy courteous mind, and all things framèd so
As answered well unto thy virtuous fame,
The gentleness that at thy hands I found
In stranger's house, all unacquainted I,

Good S., hath my heart to thee so bound,
That from thee can it not be forced to fly.
In pledge whereof, my service here I give,
If thou so wilt, to serve thee whilst I live.

42 Of Money.

Give money me, take friendship whoso list,
For friends are gone come once adversity,
When money yet remaineth safe in chest,
That quickly can thee bring from misery.
Fair face show friends, when riches do abound,
Come time of proof, farewell, they must away;
Believe me well, they are not to be found,
If God but send thee once a louring day.
Gold never starts aside, but in distress
Finds ways enough to ease thine heaviness.

43 Going towards Spain.

Farewell, thou fertile soil,
 that Brutus first out found,
When he, poor soul, was driven clean
 from out his country ground;
That northward lay'st thy lusty sides
 amid the raging seas,
Whose wealthy land doth foster up
 thy people all in ease,
While others scrape and cark abroad,
 their simple food to get,
And seely souls take all for good
 that cometh to the net,
Which they with painful pains do pinch
 in barren burning realms,
While we have all without restraint
 among thy wealthy streams.
O blessed of God, thou pleasant isle,
 where wealth herself doth dwell,
Wherein my tender years I passed,
 I bid thee now farewell.
For fancy drives me forth abroad,

and bids me take delight
In leaving thee and ranging far,
to see some stranger sight,
And saith I was not framèd here
to live at home with ease,
But passing forth for knowledge sake
to cut the foaming seas.

44 At Bonneval in France.

O fond affection, wounder of my heart,
When wilt thou cease to breed my restless pain?
When comes the end of this my cruel smart?
When shall my force beat back thy force again?
When shall I say this restless rage of mine,
By reason ruled, is banished quite away,
And I escaped these cruel bonds of thine,
O flaming fiend, that seekest my decay?
Safe thinking I, Charybdis' rage to fly,
On Scylla rock, in Bonneval I die.

45 Coming homeward out of Spain.

O raging seas, and mighty Neptune's reign,
In monstrous hills that throwest thyself so high,
That with thy floods dost beat the shores of Spain,
And break the cliffs, that dare thy force envy,
Cease now thy rage and lay thine ire aside;
And Thou that hast the governance of all,
O mighty God, grant weather, wind, and tide,
Till on my country coast, our anchor fall.

46 To L. Blundeston of Ingratitude.

The little bird, the tender marlion,
That useth oft upon the lark to prey,
With great reproach doth stain the mind of man,
If all be true that writers of her say.
For she, a creature maimed of reason's part,
And framed to live according to her kind,
Doth seem to foster reason in her heart,

And to aspire unto diviner mind.
When hunger's rage she hath exilèd quite,
And suppèd well as falleth for her state,
The seely lark doth take by force of flight,
And hies to tree whereas she lodgèd late,
And on the trembling bird all night she stands,
To keep her feet from force of nipping cold.
The amazèd wretch, within her enemy's hands
And closèd fast within the clasping hold,
Awaiteth death with drowsy drooping heart,
And all the night with fear draws on her life.
The gentle bird, when darkness doth depart,
Doth not deprive the seely soul of life,
Nor fills with her, her hungered eager breast,
But weighing well the service she hath done,
To spill the blood her nature doth detest,
And from so great a crime herself doth shun.
She lets her go; and more, with steadfast eyes
Beholds which way she takes with mazèd flight,
And in those parts that day she never flies,
Lest on that bird again she chance to light.
Lo, Blund'ston, here, how kindness doth abound
In seely souls where reason is exiled.
This bird alone sufficeth to confound
The brutish minds of men that are defiled
With that great vice, that vile and heinous crime,
Ingratitude (which some unkindness call),
That poison strong that springeth still with time,
Till at the length, it hath infected all.

***46a** The Answer of L. Blundeston to the same.

This mirror left of this thy bird, I find
Hath not such force to enter in the heart
To root away unthankfulness of mind,
As others have, the virtues to pervert,
(so prone we are to vice).
The tench by kind hath salve for every sore,
And heals the maimèd pike in his distress;
The churlish pike for gentleness therefore,
In his reward doth cruelly express

His murd'ring mind, his filthy spotted faith:
When hunger pricks to fill his greedy jaws,
He grips his poor chirurgeon unto death,
Who late to him of life was only cause.
Thy marlions have few aeries in our ground,
But pikes have spawns good store in every pound.

47 To the tune of Appelles.

The rushing rivers that do run,
The valleys sweet, adornèd new,
That leans their sides against the sun,
With flowers fresh of sundry hue,
Both ash and elm, and oak so high,
Do all lament my woeful cry.

While winter black, with hideous storms
Doth spoil the ground of summer's green,
While springtime sweet the leaf returns
That late on tree could not be seen,
While summer burns, while harvest reigns,
Still, still, do rage my restless pains.

No end I find in all my smart,
But endless torment I sustain
Since first, alas, my woeful heart
By sight of thee was forced to plain.
Since that I lost my liberty,
Since that thou mad'st a slave of me,

My heart that once abroad was free,
Thy beauty hath in durance brought.
Once reason ruled and guided me,
And now is wit consumed with thought;
Once I rejoiced above the sky,
And now for thee, alas, I die;

Once I rejoiced in company,
And now my chief and whole delight
Is from my friends away to fly
And keep alone my wearied sprite:
Thy face divine and my desire

From flesh hath me transformed to fire.

O Nature, thou that first did frame
My lady's hair of purest gold,
Her face of crystal to the same,
Her lips of precious ruby's mould,
Her neck of alablaster white,
Surmounting far each other wight,

Why didst thou not that time devise?
Why didst thou not foresee before
The mischief that thereof doth rise,
And grief on grief doth heap with store,
To make her heart of wax alone,
And not of flint and marble stone?

O lady, show thy favour yet,
Let not thy servant die for thee;
Where rigour ruled, let mercy sit;
Let pity conquer cruelty.
Let not disdain, a fiend of hell,
Possess the place where grace should dwell.

CUPIDO CONQUERED

48 Cupido Conquered.

The sweetest time of all the year
    it was, whenas the sun
Had newly entered Gemini,
    and warming heat begun,
When every tree was clothèd green,
    and flowers fair did show,
And when the white and blooming may
    on hawthorns thick did grow,
When sore I longed to seek abroad
    to see some pleasant sight
Amid my woes and heavy haps
    that might my mind delight.
Care would not let me bide within,
    but forced me forth to go,
And bade me seek some present help
    for to relieve my woe.
Then forward went I forth in haste
    to view the garnished trees,
What time the sun was mounted up
    twixt nine and ten degrees.
From flowers flew sweet airs abroad,
    delighting much my brain;
With sight and smells gan sorrow fade,
    and joy return again,
So that in mind I much rejoice
    to feel myself so light,
For gorgeous sights and odours sweet
    had new revived my sprite.

Beside the pleasant harmony
that singing birds did make
Bade me pull up my heart again,
and sorrow soon forsake.
'For though,' quoth Reason, 'she be gone
on whom thy life depends,
'Yet fond it is to cark and care
where there is none amends.'
Thus forth I went, and in the groves
I rangèd here and there,
Whereas I heard such pleasant tunes
as heaven had been near.
I think that if Amphion had
been present there to play,
Or if Sir Orpheus might have held
his harp that present day,
Or if Apollo with his lute
had striven to excel,
None of them all by music should
have borne away the bell.
I rather judge the Thracian would
his harp wherewith he played
Have cast away, as one whom ire
had utterly dismayed.
Such passing tunes of sundry birds
I never heard before;
The further I went in the woods,
the noise resounded more.
'O happy birds,' quoth I, 'what life
is this that you do lead?
'How far from care and misery?
how far from fear and dread?
'With what rejoicing melody
pass you this fading life,
'While man, unhappiest creature, lives
in wretched toil and strife.'
Still forth I went, and wondered at
this pleasant harmony,
And gazèd at these little fools
that made such melody,
Till at the length I gan to spy

a stately laurel tree,
So placed and set in such a guise,
that as it seemed to me,
Dame Nature strove to show herself
in planting such a thing;
For even out beside the rock
a fountain clean did spring,
Where in the water I beheld,
resembled wondrous true,
The white and green of all the trees,
adornèd late of new,
And how in order eke they stood,
a goodly sight to see,
And there I might discern the birds
that sung in every tree,
To move the bill and shake the wings
in uttering music sweet,
And here and there to fly to feed,
and eftsoons there to meet.
Great pleasure had I there to bide,
and stare upon the spring,
For why? methought it did surmount
each other kind of thing.
Now was the sun got up aloft,
and raught the middle line,
And in the well, the golden globe
with flaming beams did shine,
Whereof the brightness was so great
that I might not endure
Longer to look within the spring,
whose waters were so pure.
Unwilling went I thence away,
and underneath the tree
I laid me down, whose branches broad
did keep the sun from me,
Thinking to rest me there a while,
till falling some degrees,
Sir Phoebus should have hid himself
behind the shadowing trees,
And then for to have viewed the spring,
and markèd every place,

And seen if there I could have spied
the weeping Byblis' face.
For sure I think it was the place
wherein Narcissus died,
Or else the well to which was turned
poor Byblis while she cried.
But whether it was weariness,
with labour that I took,
Or fume that from the spring did rise,
wherein I late did look,
Or if it were the sweet accord
that singing birds did keep,
Or what it was, I know no whit,
but I fell fast asleep.
I think the woody nymphs agreed
that I should have this chance,
And that it was their pleasure so
to show me things in trance.
Whilst I lay thus in slumber deep,
I might perceive to stand
A person clothèd all in white,
that held a rod in hand,
Which was, methought, of massy gold;
I knew it very well,
For that was it, made Argus sleep,
while he did Io steal.
When I perceived by his attire
that it was Mercury,
My heart at first began to faint;
yet at the length quoth I,
'Thou goddess' son, why stand'st thou there,
what business now with thee?
'What meanest thou in thy flying weed
for to appear to me?'
And therewithal my thought I stayed,
and could no farther speak,
For fear did force my speech to fail,
and courage waxèd weak.
Which when the son of Maia saw,
he took me by the hand,
'Look up,' quoth he, 'be not afraid,

but boldly by me stand.
'The Muses all of Helicon
have sent me now to thee,
'Whom thou dost serve and whose thou seek'st
for evermore to be.
'And thanks to thee by me they send,
because thou tookest pain
'In their affairs (a thankless thing)
to occupy thy brain,
'Desiring thee not for to stay
for Momus' ill report,
'But ending that thou hast begun,
to spite the cankered sort.
'And think not thou, that thou art he
that canst escape disdain;
'The day shall come when thankful men
shall well accept thy pain,
'But rather lay before thine eyes
the high attempts of those
'Whose stately style with painful proof
their worthy wits disclose.
'Mark him that thundered out the deeds
of old Anchises' son,
'Whose English verse gives Maro's grace
in all that he hath done,
'Whose death the Muses sorrow much,
that lack of agèd days
'Amongst the common Britons old,
should hinder Virgil's praise.
'Mark him that hath well framed a glass
for states to look upon,
'Whose labour shows the ends of them
that livèd long agone.
'Mark him that shows the tragedies,
thine own familiar friend,
'By whom the Spaniard's haughty style
in English verse is penned.
'Mark these same three, and other moe,
whose doings well are known,
'Whose fair attempts in every place
the flying fame hath blown.

'Hast thou not heard, thyself in place
full oft and many a time,
'"Lo, here the author loseth grace,
lo, here a doltish rhyme;"
'Now sith that they have this reward
who pass thee even as far
'As in the night Diana doth
excel the dimmest star,
'Take thou no scorn at evil tongues:
what need'st thou to disdain?
'Sith they whom none can well amend
have like fruit of their pain.
'Moreover yet the ladies nine
have all commanded me,
'Because they know the blinded god
hath something piercèd thee,
'To lead thee forth, a thing to see,
if all things happen right,
'Which shall give thee occasion good,
with joyful mind to write.'
To this, I would have answered fain
and there began to speak,
But as my words were coming forth
my purpose he did break.
'Come on,' quoth he, 'none answer now;
we may no longer stay,
'But frame thyself to fly abroad,
for hence we must away.'
And here withal, on both my sides,
two wings methought did grow
Of mighty breadth; away went he,
and after him I flow.
And ever as we mounted up,
I looked upon my wings,
And proud I was, methought, to see
such unacquainted things.
Till forth we flew, my guide and I,
with mounting flight apace,
Beholding rivers, woods, and hills,
and many a goodly place,
Till at the length methought I might

a gorgeous castle spy.
There down began my guide to fall,
and downward eke fell I:
'Lo, here the place where thou must light,'
gan Mercury to say,
'Farewell, and note what thou dost see,
for I must hence away.'
And with this same away flew he,
and left me there alone,
Whereas with fear amazed I stood,
and thus began to moan:
'Alas, where am I now become,
what cursèd chance hath blown
'Me from the place where I was bred,
to countries here unknown?
'What meant that fell unhappy fiend,
that Maia brought to light,
'To bring me from my heart's desire,
to see this doleful sight?
'Unhappy wretch, I would I had
his person here in hand!
'Then should I wreak mine ire of him
that brought me to this land.
'But all too late, alas, I wish,
for words avail not now;
''Tis best to learn what place it is,
and yet I know not how.
'Alas, that here were Ptolemy,
with compass globe in hand,
'Whose art should show me true the place
and climate where I stand.
'Well yet whatsoever chance thereon,
whatsoever realm it be,
'Yon castle will I visit sure,
hap what hap will to me.'
Thus much methought alone I spoke,
and then I forward went,
And cursèd eke a hundredfold
them that me thither sent.
Thus to the castle straight I came,
which when I viewed about

And saw the workmanship thereof
full gorgeously set out,
I entered in, with fearful heart,
much doubting how to speed,
But ever hope of happy chance
my heavy heart did feed.
Wide was the court and large within,
the walls were raisèd high
And all engraved with stories fair
of costly imagery.
There might I see, with wondrous art,
the picture portured plain
Of old Orion, hunter good,
whom scorpions vile had slain,
And by him stood his boarspear and
his other instruments,
His net, his dart, his courser, and
his hunter's resting tents,
And under him was written fair,
in letters all of gold,
Here lies he slain with scorpion's sting,
unhappy wretch, that would
Have forced the lady of this fort,
with stain of royalty,
To have consented to his will
in filthy lechery.
Wherefore beware that enters here,
whatsoever man thou art;
Account thyself but lost, if that
thou bear'st a lecherous heart.
When I had viewed these written lines
and marked the story well,
I joyèd much, for why I knew
Diana there did dwell;
Diana, she that goddess is
of virgin's sacred mind,
By whom Orion, hunter wild,
his fatal end did find.
Next unto him I might behold
Acteon, woeful wight;
In what a manner, all totorn,

his cruel dogs him dight,
There might be seen, their greedy mouths
with master's blood imbrued,
And all his own unhappy men
that fast their lord pursued.
And many stories more there were
engraved, too long to tell,
What fearful haps to many men
for lust unclean befell.
Thus as I stood with musing mind
beholding all things there,
In rusheth at the gate behind
a post, with heavy cheer.
Into the hall with haste he hies,
and after followed I
To hear what kind of news he brought
or what he meant thereby.
He, passing through the hall in haste,
at entrance never stayed,
But blowing fast for want of breath,
as one almost dismayed,
Approached in presence to the sight
of chaste Diana's face,
That all encompassed round about
with virgins in that place,
In lofty chair of high estate
did sit, all clothed in white
Of silver hue, that shining gave,
methought, a gorgeous sight.
There did I see fair Dido Queen,
and fair Hypsipyle,
And next to them Lucretia sat,
and chaste Penelope.
But these same four no bows did bear,
for virgin's sacred state
They had forsaken long ago
and joined with faithful mate.
On the other side, sat all the sort
of fair Diana's train
Whose trade with toil amongst the woods
was ever bent to pain,

Whose sacred minds were ne'er defiled
with any wanton lust,
Which never could the fickle state
of lovers' fancy trust.
The chief of them was Ismenis,
whom best Diana loved,
And next in place sat Hyale,
whom never fancy moved,
Next unto them sat Niphe fair,
a gem of chastity,
And next to her sat Phiale,
not basest in degree;
Behind them all, of passing form,
fair Rhanis held her place,
And nigh to her I might discern
Dame Psecas' shining face.
These princely nymphs accompanèd
Diana in her bains,
Whileas in shape of stag, poor wretch,
Acteon had his pains.
Above them all I might behold,
as placed before the rest,
Hippolytus, whom Phaedra's spite
most cruelly had dressed,
Hippolytus, the unspotted pearl
of pure virginity,
Whose noble heart could not agree
to stepdame's villainy.
Next unto him sat Continence,
and next was Labour placed:
Of body big and strong he was,
and somewhat crabtree faced.
Next him was placèd Abstinence,
a lean unwieldy wight,
Whose diet thin had banished clean
all fond and vain delight.
A thousand more methought there were
whose names I did not know,
And if I did, too long it were
in verses them to show.
Down of his knees the messenger

before them all doth fall,
And unto chaste Diana there
for succour thus doth call:
'O Goddess chief of chastity,
and sacred virgin's mind,
'Let pity from your noble heart
redress for misers find.
'Let not our wearied hearts sustain
such wrongful tyranny!
'Quench quickly now the fiery flames
of open injury.'
This said, for fear he stayed a while,
and then began again:
'A mighty prince,' quoth he, 'is come
with great unruly train,
'All armèd well at every point
(A dreadful sight to see),
'And every man in feats of arms,
right skillful all they be.
'The captain chief in chariot ride
with pomp and stately pride,
'With bow in hand of glistering gold,
and quiver by his side,
'Where many a shaft full sharp doth lie,
and many a mortal dart,
'That hath with poisoned force destroyed
full many a yielding heart.
'He entered hath within your realm,
and taken many a fort,
'Hath sacked them all, and spoiled them quite,
and slain a wondrous sort
'In strangest guise, for where he shoots
the wound doth fester still,
'And all the surgeons that we have
cannot remove the ill.
'In little time the grief so sore
doth grow in every part,
'Distraining through the venomed veins,
doth so torment the heart
'That some to rid themselves thereof
in floods full deep they leap

'And drown themselves; some downward falls
from houses high by heap;
'Some anchor cast on crossèd beams
to rid themselves from strife,
'And hang themselves full thick on trees
to end a wretched life.
'And they whose fearful minds dare not
thus make an end of woe,
'With grievous flames, consuming long,
their life at length forgo.
'Lo, here the sum of all I have:
this tiger us annoys,
'And cruelly hath spoilèd us
of all our wonted joys,
'Whom if your Grace do not repulse
and find some present stay,
'Undoubtedly he will win this realm,
and take us all away.'
At this, the ladies all amazed
for fear did look full pale,
And all beheld with mazèd eyes
the wretch that told the tale.
Till at the length Hippolytus
of heart and courage high,
Nothing abashed with sudden news,
began thus to reply:
'Cast fear away, fair dames,' quoth he,
'dismay yourselves no more;
'I know by whom this mischief springs
and know a help therefor.
'It is not such a dreadful wight
as he doth here report
'That entered is within these parts
and plagues the simple sort.
'Nor is his force so great to fear:
I know it, I, full well.
'It is the scornful blinded boy,
that near to us doth dwell,
'Whom Mars long time ago begot
of that lascivious dame,
'That linked in chains for lechery,

received an open shame;
'A disobedient blinded fool
that durst presume to turn
'His darts against his mother once,
and caused her sore to burn,
'An ancient foe to all this Court
of long time he hath been,
'And hath attempted evermore
by this renown to win.
'His cruel heart, of pity void,
doth spare no kind of age,
'But tender youth and doting age
he strikes in furious rage,
'And laughs to scorn the seely souls
that he hath wounded so,
'No fine appointed of their ills,
no end of all their woe.
'But since he hath presumèd thus
to enter here in place,
'And here to threaten conquests thus
against Diana's Grace,
'Let him be sure his lofty mind
this deed shall soon repent,
'If that your Grace do here agree
with free and full consent
'To make me chieftain of this charge
and whom I list to choose,
'If prisoner here I bring him not,
let me mine honour lose.'
And there he ceased with joyful looks;
the ladies smilèd all,
And thorough his words they hopèd soon
to see Cupido's fall.
With heavenly voice Diana there,
as chief above the rest,
This wise her words began to frame
from out her sacred breast:
'My good Hippolytus,' quoth she,
'whose true and faithful mind
'In doubtful danger often I
do always ready find

'For to revenge the cankered rage
of all my spiteful foes,
'Thou he from whose unspotted heart
the floods of virtue flows,
'Whose service long hath been approved
within this Court of mine,
'Restrain this boy's unruly rage
by valiant means of thine.
'I give thee leave, and thee appoint
my chief lieutenant here,
'Choose whom thou wilt, take whom thou list,
thou needest no whit to fear.'
With this he rose from out his place,
and looking round about,
Chose Abstinence and Continence,
with Labour, captain stout.
And with these three he took his leave
of all the ladies there,
Who, doubting of his safe return,
let fall full many a tear.
He left them there in heaviness,
and made no more delay,
But outward went and toward the camp
he took the nearest way.
With this the Queen's commission straight
was sent abroad in haste
To raise up soldiers round about,
and with their captain placed,
To bring them forth and marching on,
Hippolytus to meet.
Then sounded trumpets all abroad,
and drums in every street,
And soldiers good, like swarms of bees
their captains press about,
All armèd brave in corselets white,
they march with courage stout,
And forward shove, till at the length
whereas their marshall lies,
They find the place; the joyful sounds
do mount above the skies.
Hippolytus received them all

with words of pleasant cheer,
And placeth them in good array,
because the camp was near.
Three battles big of them he frames,
and of the rearward strong
Hath Labour charge, who steppeth forth
before the stately throng,
And captain of the rearward next
was placèd Abstinence,
And joined to him for policy
was Captain Continence.
The battle main Hippolytus
himself did choose to guide,
And in the foremost front thereof
on courser fair doth ride.
The trumpets sound 'march on apace,'
and drums the same do strike.
Then forward moves the army great
in order martial-like.
I came behind (methought), and best
it seemèd then to me
To view the dint of dreadful sword,
and fighter none to be.
Three spies were sent abroad to view
the place where Cupid lay:
Alongst a river fair and broad
they spy a pleasant way,
Which way they took, and passing forth
at length appears a plain
Both large and vast, where lies the rout
of cruel Cupid's train.
Thus told the spies; we onward hie,
and straight in sight we have
The fearful show of all our foes
and dreadful army brave.
The first that marched from Cupid's camp
was drowsy Idleness,
The chiefest friend that Love had then;
the next was vile Excess,
A lubber great, misshapen most
of all that there I saw,

As much I think in quantity
as horses six can draw,
A mighty face both broad and flat,
and all with rubies set,
Much nosèd like a turkey cock,
with teeth as black as jet,
A belly big, full trussed with guts,
and pistols two, like posts,
A knave full square in every point,
a prince of drunken hosts,
Upon a camel couchèd high,
for horse could none him bear,
A mighty staff in hand he had
his foes afar to fear.
Behind them all, the blinded god
doth come in chariot fair,
With raging flames flung round about
he pesters all the air.
And after him, for triumph leads
a thousand wounded hearts
That gush abroad hot streams of blood,
new piercèd with his darts.
The army ready for to meet
and all at point to fight,
Hippolytus, with lusty cheer
and with a noble sprite,
His soldiers to encourage, thus
his words begins to place:
'My valiant friends and subjects all
of chaste Diana's Grace,
'Whose noble hearts were never stained
with spot of dastard's mind,
'Behold our enemies here at hand,
behold yon coward blind,
'Of little force compared with you,
how in a fond array
'They straggle out, no order due
observèd in their way.
'Behold what goodly guides they have
to govern them withal,
'That never knew what fighting meant,

but live to Venus thrall.
'Mark him that guides the rearward there,
that vile deformèd churl,
'Whose foggy mates with paunches side
do thick about him whirl.
'And he that foremost hither comes:
lo! what a handsome squire!
'Sure full unapt to keep the field,
more fit to sit by the fire.
'In fine, lo, victory at hand
with high triumphant crown,
'Bent for to spoil our foes of fame
and cast their glory down.
'Fight therefore now courageously,
and rid your friends of fear;
'Declare your manhood valiantly,
and let your hearts appear.'
With this the sound begins to mount
and noise high to rise,
And warlike tunes begin to dash
themselves against the skies.
The cannon's crack begins to roar,
and darts full thick they fly,
And covered thick the armies both,
and framed a counter sky.
And now the battles both be joined
with stroke of hand to try
The quarrel just, and for to find
where victory doth lie.
The soldiers all of Idleness,
where Labour comes, do fall,
And wounded sore by force of him
all bathed in blood they sprawl.
Himself alone with Idleness
now hand to hand doth fight,
And after many a mortal wound
destroys the seely wight.
Then joins with him Sir Abstinence
with aid and succours new,
And both upon the greasy host
of Gluttony they flew.

The Captain doth advance himself
with Abstinence to meet:
The unwieldy creature, smitten there,
is tumbled under feet.
Then Fancy flies, Incontinence,
and all Cupido's friends,
Beholding Fortune thus to frown
by flight themself defends.
Cupido, when he sees himself
thus spoiled of all his aid,
The chief supporters of his Court
so suddenly decayed,
Bade turn his chariots then with haste
and fast away he flies;
Amongst the chaste Hippolytus
on swifty courser hies.
Then all with joy they after run,
down thick the enemies fall;
The blinded boy for succour straight
to Venus high doth call,
But all his cries availeth not,
his foes him fast pursue;
The driver of his chariot, soon
Hippolytus there slew,
And down from horse the wretch doth fall.
The horses spoiled of guide,
A soldier stout of Reason's band
is willèd there to ride,
Who turning reins another way
restrains him of his flight.
His honours lost, and taken thus,
Cupid, in doleful plight,
These words with trembling voice began:
'Sith Fortune thus,' quoth he,
'Hath given her doom from doubtful breast
and turned her grace from me,
'Sith that the most misfortune now
that ever I could find
'Hath chanced to me, and miser I,
by Destinies assigned
'Am captive here, consider yet,

what Fortune might have wrought,
'And made a conqueror of me,
and you in bondage brought.
'Consider yet the woeful plight
wherein you had remained,
'If that the gods my happy state
had not so sore disdained.
'And by your grief, then measure mine;
show mercy in this case.
'That conqueror commended is,
who gives to pity place;
'The cruel mind dispraisèd is
in every kind of state.
'No man so haughty lives on earth,
but once may find his mate.
'These words, Hippolytus, I speak,
to breed no farther strife.
'I speak not this of malice here:
my suit is for my life.
'Sith Fortune thus hath favoured you,
grant this my small request,
'And let me live, if mercy dwell
within your noble breast.'
By this time Morpheus had dispersed
the drowsy cloud of sleep,
And from my brains the quiet trance
began full fast to creep
And downward fell. I waked therewith
and looking round about,
Long time I musèd where I was;
my mind was still in doubt.
Till at the length I viewed the tree
and place whereas I sat,
And well beheld the pleasant spring
that late I wondered at.
I saw beside the golden globe
of Phoebus shining bright,
That westward half did hide his face,
approaching fast the night.
Each bird began to shroud himself
in tree to take his rest,

And ceased the pleasant tunes that late
proceeded from their breast.
I homeward went, and left them all,
and restless all that night
I musing lay, tormented thus
with fond lamenting sprite.
When Phoebus rose, to pass the time
and pass my grief away,
I took my pen and penned the dream
that made my Muses stay.
Finis.

Selected Other Works by Googe

This addendum contains modernized transcriptions of four poems by Googe printed in 1560 in his translations of Nilus Cabasilas and Palingenius, and of the prose epistle to Sir William Cecil printed in the 1561 edition of Palingenius. The four poems make up the total of Googe's original verse besides the *Eclogues, Epitaphs, and Sonnets,* and the allegorical poem *The Ship of Safeguard* attributed to him. The epistle to Cecil presents a statement of Googe's view of the nature and purpose of poetry.

Prefatory poem from Nilus Cabasilas, *A Brief Treatise, containing a plain and fruitful declaration of the Pope's usurped Primacy, written in Greek above vii hundred years since, by Nilus, an ancient archbishop of Thessalonia, and newly translated into English by Thomas Gressop student in Oxford.* Henry Sutton for Ralph Newbery, 16 March 1560. STC 4325.

Let rancour not you rule,
O men of Romish sect:
Expel the poison from your breasts
That doth you thus infect.
Let not that haughty whore
That boasts herself for God,
That rules the realms of Caesar's right
With her usurpèd rod,
Let not this hag I say,
Bewitch your earthly eyes,
That here embraceth beastly joy
And virtue doth despise.
Antiquity, she saith,
Gave her this stately place:

Lo here Antiquity you see
Doth her and hers deface.
        Lo here doth Nilus teach,
A man of ancient time,
How much she is to be abhorred,
How much she swells with crime.
        Leave her therefore in time,
Forsake her wicked ways:
Let us and you agree in one,
So God shall have his praise.
Finis qp B.G.

The next three poems are from *The First three Books of the most Christian Poet Marcellus Palingenius, called the Zodiac of life: newly translated out of Latin into English by Barnabe Googe*. John Tisdale, for Ralph Newbery, 1560. STC 19148.

The Preface.

Whenas Sir Phebe with backward course
        the hornèd Goat had caught,
And had the place from whence he turns
        his lofty face out-sought
Amid the entrance of the grades
        of Capricorn he stood,
And distant far from him away
        was Mars with fiery mood,
He lacked th'aspect of mighty Jove
        and Venus' pleasant look;
With beams he could not broil from high,
        for heat his globe forsook.
Old Saturn then aloft did lie,
        with rusty rivelled face,
And with a backward course he ran
        from out the Twins apace,
And towards the Bull he gan to drive,
        intending there to rest
His crooked crabbèd cankered limbs
        in lovely Venus' nest.
With frozen face about he looked
        and vile deformèd hue,

And down the boisterous Boreas sent
    in every coast that blew:
Who spoiled the pleasant trees of leaf,
    bereft the ground of green,
That life in springing sprigs or plants
    might nowhere now be seen.
The lively sap forsook the bough
    and deep the root it held,
And spoiling fruits, the flaky snows
    on tender boughs they dwelled.
When down amongst my books I sat
    and close I crouched for cold,
Fair ladies nine with stately steps
    aloof I might behold,
In mantles girt of comely grace
    and books in hand they bare,
With laurel wreath their heads were crowned,
    a sight to me but rare.
I saw them come and up I rose,
    as duty moved, to meet
These learned nymphs, and down I fall
    before their comely feet.
With rosy lips and shining face
    and Melpomen her name,
This Lady first began to speak
    and thus her words to frame:
'Stand up, young man,' quoth she, 'dispatch,
    and take thy pen in hand,
'Write thou the Civil wars and broil
    in ancient Latins' land.
'Reduce to English sense,' she said,
    'the lofty Lucan's verse,
'The cruel chance and doleful end
    of Caesar's state rehearse.'
'Madam,' quoth Urany, 'with that,
    in this you do me wrong,
'To move my man to serve your turn,
    that hath professed of long
'And vowed his years with me to serve
    in secret motions high,
'To beat his brain in searching forth

the rollings of the sky.
'Nay, rather take in hand,' quod she,
(and on me full she looks)
'With English rhyme to bring to light
Aratus' worthy books.
'Describe the whirling spheres above
and movings every one,
'How forced about from East to West,
from West to East they gone.
'Aratus' verse will shew thee plain
how circles all they run,
'How glides the course thorough crooked line
of Phebe the shining Sun;
'Whereas the fixèd Poles do stay,
and where the Snake doth creep,
'In heavens high, amid the north
where Bears their course do keep.
'By this,' quod she, 'thou shalt receive
immortal fame at last,
'Much more than if thou should'st declare
those bloody banquets past.'
These words declared with pleasant voice,
this Lady held her peace,
And forth before them all I saw
the loveliest Lady press:
Of stature tall, and Venus face
she seemed methought to have,
And Calliope she callèd was
with verse that writes so grave.
'Sisters,' quod she, 'and Ladies all
of Jove his mighty line,
'To whom no art doth lie unhid
that here we may define,
'Chief patrons of the Poets poor,
and aiders of their verse,
'Without whose help their simple heads
would nothing well rehearse,
'I am become a suitor here
to you my Ladies all,
'For him that here before you stands
as unto learning thrall.

'A Poet late I had whose pen
did tread the crabbèd ways
'Of virtuous life, declaring how
that men should spend their days.
'In Romish land he livèd long,
and Palingen his name
'It was: whereby he got himself
an everlasting fame
'Of them that learnèd be. But of
the mean and ruder sort
'He lives unknown, and lacks thereby
his just and right report.
'Wherefore my suit is to you all,
grant me this wight a while
'That standeth here, that he may turn
my Poet's stately style
'To vulgar speech in native tongue,
that all may understand.'
To this they all agreed, and said,
'Take thou that work in hand.'
Amazèd then I answered thus:
'Good Ladies all,' quoth I,
'Whose clients' fame for ever flies
and name can never die,
'Return your sentence late pronounced,
call back your words again,
'And let not me take that in hand
that I cannot attain.
'In England here a hundred heads
more able now there be
'This same to do: then choose the best
and let the worst go free.
'Best you do so than that my verse
receive immortal shame,
'When I shall pay the price of pains
with hazard of my name.'
With this they all began to frown
and wholly with one voice,
'Take thou this same in hand,' they cry,
'thou hast none other choice.'
And fast away from me they fling,

as half in angry mood.
They left me thus in woeful case,
whereas a while I stood,
And musèd what I best might do;
at last my pen I took,
Commanded thus to english here
this famous Poet's book.
Now since that I have thus begun,
you, learnèd, I require
With your dispraise or great disdain
quench not this kindled fire,
But give me rather cause to end
this work so late begun:
So shall I think are well bestowed
my pains when all is done.

The Book to the reader.

Who seeks to shun the shatt'ring sails
of mighty Momus' mast,
Must not attempt the sugared seas
where Muses anchor cast.
For Momus there doth ride at float,
with scornful tongues yfreight:
With cankered cracks of wrathful words
he keeps the passage strait,
That none without disdain may pass
where Muses' navy lies,
But straight on them with ireful mood,
the scornful God he flies.
Since none may scape, I am not he
that can myself assure
Through surging seas of deep disdain
my passage to procure,
But am content for to receive
reproach at Momus' hand,
Sith none there is that may the nose
of Rhinocere withstand.
The learnèd wits I here require
with rigour not to judge:
The common sort I nought esteem,

unskilful though they grudge,
Nor few of them can hold their peace
but find themselves ado
I[n] viewing works as he that sought
to mend Appelles' shoe.
Both sorts I wish if that they would
contented to remain,
And bear the weakness of my wit,
and not thereat disdain.

The Translator to the Reader.

If Chaucer now should live,
Whose eloquence divine
Hath passed the poets all that came
Of ancient Brutus' line;
If Homer here might dwell,
Whose praise the Greeks resound;
If Virgil might his years renew;
If Ovid might be found:
All these might well be sure
Their matches here to find,
So much doth England flourish now
With men of Muses' kind.
Since these might find their mates,
What shame shall this my rhyme
Receive that thus I publish here
In such a parlous time?
A Poet once there lived,
And Cheril was his name,
Who thought of Alexander's acts
To make immortal fame.
Bred up in Pegase' house,
Of Poets' ancient blood,
A thousand verses ill he made,
And none but seven good.
Sith Homer, Virgil, and the rest
May here their matches see,
Let Cheril not thereat disdain:
He shall be matched with me.
For each good verse he did receive

A piece of gold, I trow;
For each ill verse the king did bid
His ear should feel a blow.
Though I presume with him as mate
Coequal to remain,
Yet seek I not herein to be
Coparcener of his gain.
FINIS

The following is the dedicatory epistle from *The first six books of the most Christian Poet Marcellus Palingenius, called the Zodiac of life ... translated ... by Barnabe Googe*. John Tisdale, for Rafe Newbery, 1561. STC 19149.

To the right honourable and his singular good Master, Sir William Cecil, Knight. One of the most honourable Privy Council, Master of the Wards, and Liveries, and Secretary to the Queen's highness. Barnabe Googe wisheth long life, with increase of honour.

Evidently it appeareth, right honourable sir, that all diseases, the more fervent they be, the greater and stronger medicines they require; and each fire, the fiercer the flame doth rage the more water is requisite to the quenching thereof. Whereby it doth follow, that vice and evil life (being a sickness of all sickness, extremest: so much that by it is corrupted both body and soul, and a fire so fervent, that thereunto no fire may be compared, a fire, I say, consuming both hope of life hereafter to be had, and also destroying virtue, honest deeds, and godly minds, the perfect and true beauty of man in this life) requireth medicines of greatest force to the purging thereof, and whole fountains of virtuous writings to the extinguishing of the same.

Now, seeing that writers are the only means whereby this corrupting sore may be remedied, at the leastwise greatly allayed, then ought we to have those writers in most reputation, honour, and remembrance, whose famous force hath best prevailed in remedying of the aforesaid inconvenience. But two only sorts of writers (all men knows) there be, whereby this act is performed, the one writing in prose, the other in verse. Of these two whose force is greatest in persuading I think no man doth doubt, conferring the plain and smooth style of the one with the haughty and heavenly style of the other. For the force, I would wish them to consider the example of Hipponax and Bubalus, and also the story of Tirtaeus the lame Poet, written at large in Justin, which both examples (because I think them frivolous to recite unto your honour, and yet necessary for the ignorant) I have here left them out and registered them in mine Alphabet of Poetical words.

But now to my first intent. Worthily have the first sort attempted to give this remedy and minister this medicine.

But most worthily hath the second profited in the abating of this fire and assuaging of this flame. For what vice so odious can be remembered, or what crime so detestable may be reported, that they with sugared sentences have not assaulted, with godly instructions battered, and thundering words exiled? Again, what virtue remains there to be told of, or good order of life to be used, that they have not highly commended, worthily extolled, and perfectly taught? In so much that I think verily, the almighty God hath ordained them in all ages to extol virtue, and rebuke vice: as the divine Plato (although a judge something too severe against them) in his book *De Furore Poetico* doth confess. Some men perchance will say they are not so much to be commended as I here affirm, but rather to be dispraised because in all their writings they have uttered strange fancies and monstrous lies, yea and many of their works have swarmed with naughty and filthy tales. To whom I answer, that as they so did, so were they by necessity constrained; for the people at that time (as now but much more worse) were so loath to read anything that rebuked vice and so negligent of virtuous exhortations that (no remedy) they were enforced to use such sweet delighting fancies, as the Physician doth sugar for speedier receiving of bitter medicines. But what mean I thus to run at large, not considering to whom I write? Your honour may judge that through praising and commending of Poets I am rather entered into a Poet's fury. What need I to speak any more in their commendation, sith the divine Poesies of Homer, the prudent persuasions of Virgil, Horace, and Ovid, the virtuous verses of Lucretius, and last of all (yet chiefest) the Christian and heavenly style of Palingenius do sufficiently set forth the glory and praise of Poets? Which Poet for his virtuous works and godly zeal with no little labour of mine, though rudely translated, I here give unto your honour, as parcel of my service, token of my good will, and a knowledgement of my duty.

Humbly requesting that through your honour's learned protection and grave authority, the simple fruits of a young head may strongly be defended from the severe reprehensions of Momus and the malicious judgements of Zoilus, whereby the common people shall not only receive a great commodity, but also I receive greater encouraging to the finishing (at all times) of the like attempts. And thus desiring your honour to take in good part the negligence of my printer, the oversight of myself, and the rudeness of my verse, committing your honour with my good Lady and Mistress to the tuition of Him that guides the world, I end.

From Staple Inn the iii. Ides of January.
Your honour's humble servant
Barnabe Googe.

Commentary, Textual Appendix, Works Cited, Indexes

Commentary

Unless otherwise stated, all definitions of the meanings of words are taken from OED (adopting its abbreviation *a* for *ante* and † to mark an obsolete sense), and all translations of classical texts from editions in the Loeb Classical Library. The poems and epistle not written by Googe are identified by an asterisk preceding the numbering, which has been supplied by the editor.

TITLE *Eclogues, Epitaphs, and Sonnets*
Crinò notes that Spenser's use of *sonet* in the December eclogue 15 ('if I ever sonet song') is paralleled by Googe's use of 'Sonettes' as the title for his poems (366). See also Introduction p 23.

*1 Alexander Neville.
Neville (1544–1614) was Googe's cousin. See Introduction pp 6–8.
1–12 Neville is borrowing his own translation of Seneca's *Oedipus* (8–9): 'the mountains huge and high, / the blust'ring winds withstand, / And craggy rocks, the belching floods / do dash and beat from land' ([London 1563] A1).
14 *framèd*: neatly composed, well devised
15 *momish*: carpingly critical; in the spirit of Momus, god of censure and ridicule (see 39 below).
33 *crabsnouted*: ugly and ill-tempered looking; crabfaced (see 45). OED connects both these words with the crustacean rather than the sour wild apple: Neville is cited for each.
39 *Momus*: 'The carping God of reprehension, son of Nox and Somnus, whose property it is (as poets feign) never to do or make anything himself, but with curious eyes to behold the doings of other: and if anything were let pass, to carp the same. Whereof all curious carpers of other men's doings are called *Momi*' (Cooper; see 15 above).

45 *cankered*: malignant, envious
45 *carlish*: churlish, mean
45 *chuffs*: rustics, but as OED notes, 'Generally applied opprobiously, with a fitting epithet, to any person disliked,' especially 'a rude coarse churlish fellow.'
57 *the Furies*: the three vengeful deities, the Eumenides. According to Cooper, 'Poets feigned that these furies dwelled in hell: but the meaning of old writers was, that they were nothing but the wringings, torments, and gnawings of ill consciences that vexed naughty men.' Neville's argument appears to be that envy of Googe is behaviour that will invite the punishments of the Furies.
8003OED0110062 *ever-during*: everlasting
64 *peise*: weight, burden
66 *freight*: laden
75 *Misanthropoi*: misanthropes: the word is printed in Greek characters in the 1563 text; nevertheless Neville's line is cited by OED (under 'misanthrope') as the first usage.
76 *squint-eyed*: OED cites this line for the first allusive or figurative use of the word; the first recorded use of the literal sense is Puttenham (1589).
77 *leave sow to swill*: This has a proverbial ring, but does not appear in ODEP under *swill*, *sow*, *swine*, *pig*, or *hog*. The first recorded date for *swill* in this sense is according to OED *a*1570. The sentiment and tone recall Spenser's 'Let *Grill* be *Grill*, and have his hoggish mind' (*FQ* II xii 87.8).
101 *Not he that saith*: proverbial; see ODEP 192 and Tilley D402, and related proverbs.

2 To the right worshipful M. William Lovelace …
See Introduction pp 5–10. As C.T. Prouty notes, Lovelace had Canterbury as well as London connections, being 'Archbishop Parker's counsel-in-law, as well as steward of the liberties of the Cathedral of Canterbury' (34). See also Douthwaite.
1 *How loath I have been*: See Introduction pp 14, 19 and Textual Appendix pp 192–6.
6 *grossness*: lack of refinement, coarseness
22 *all together*: printed 'all togyther' in the 1563 edition; it is possible to read 'altogether,' meaning that Googe gave them to the printer entirely unpolished, rather than unpolished and all in one bundle at the same time.
26 *paper provided*: See Textual Appendix p 193.

31–2 *iam … domi*: See Martial *Epigrams* I iii 12: 'yet you might have been safer at home.'
38 *presently*: at this time. According to OED this use, common in dialects and in the US, has been obsolete in literary English since the seventeenth century.
41 *Dream*: 'Cupido Conquered'; Googe's form of reference shows his consciousness of genre.

*3 L. Blundeston to the Reader.
F.B. Williams conjectures that Blundeston is the same man who appears as Blunston in Venn (19). Venn records that Laurence Blunston or Blonston matriculated as pensioner from Christ's College in Cambridge in May of 1554 (Googe matriculated as pensioner from Christ's in May 1555; see *Alumni Cantabrigienses* I i).
1 *painted*: ornamented with the colours of rhetoric; the word carries a suggestion of speciousness or flattery.
3 *sunbeams gives*: The third person plural in -s is, according to E.A. Abbott, 'extremely common' in the sixteenth century (235–6).
13–14 *floods of the one … ebbs of the other*: No abundance (floods) of rhetorical skill in himself nor lack (ebbs) of good sense in the reader.
26 *where the power faileth*: Compare the proverb 'Take the will for the deed' (*ODEP* 890; Tilley W393).
27–8 *Colonus' radish root*: The Latin word Colonus means a farmer. The reference is to an anecdote told of Louis XI of France. Thomas Howell uses the same anecdote less elliptically in the dedicatory epistle of his *Newe Sonets and Pretie Pamphlets* (112): 'Though they be in deede bare toyes of small effecte, yet take them as chearefull as Lewis once King of Fraunce, accepted the hartie gift of a poore man, but a rude present for a Prince, being only a slender Radish roote, which he yet (considering not the value of the root but the good will of the gever rooted in his hart) highly esteemed before all other costly juels.' The anecdote, contrasting the radish of the rustic and the splendid horse given by a hopeful courtier, is succinctly quoted by Lycosthenes (*Apophthegmata* 127) under 'De beneficio dignis collato, et dignis accipiendo' (Of benefits worthily given and worthily received), citing Corrozet's *Divers Propos Memorables* as his source. The 1602 English translation of Corrozet's *Memorable Conceits of divers noble and famous personages of Christendom, of this our modern time*, gives the lengthy 'history of a Radish,' where the poor man is given a thousand crowns for his radish, and the courtier is then given this very ex-

pensive radish as recompense for his horse! The moral drawn is: 'This was a most royal kind of liberality, in recompensing bountifully the good affections and long travels of a poor man well deserving: and to reward the audacious according to his demerits' (230). See also references in Jasper Heywood's dedicatory verses to Sir John Mason, prefixed to his translation of Seneca's *Thyestes* (1560), and in Thomas Newton's dedicatory epistle to the Marquis of Winchester, prefixed to his translation of Cicero's *The worthy book of old age* (1569).

28 *barbed*: caparisoned with a barb or bard, which is 'a covering for the breast and flanks of a war-horse, originally protective, but sometimes merely ornamental'

43–4 *the xxvii of May, 1562*: On the date of Googe's return from Spain, see Sheidley (1981) 21, Eccles 359, and the Textual Appendix p 193.

4 The Preface of L. Blundeston.

The allegory of Blundeston's poem is based on medieval and renaissance psychology. Bartholomaeus Anglicus's encyclopedia *De proprietatibus rerum*, especially Book III chapters 9–11, provides the background. The 'soul sensible' gives feeling, and has the double capacity of apprehending and moving. It is divided into inner and outer wit; the inner wit is divided into three cells, containing the three virtues 'Imaginativa,' 'Estimativa,' and 'Memorativa,' Blundeston's Fancy, Reason, and Memory. Blundeston's sensible soul is dulled by overworking the brain. His outer wit could be refreshed by a walk in the country, but his inner wit is not contented with this solution. The first of the triumvirate of the inner wit (Spenser's three honourable sages in *FQ* II 9 47), Fancy, recommends recreating himself with the toys of her devise, but Reason prudently cautions against risking publishing these works of the imagination. Memory proposes a compromise solution, to print the delightful verses of Googe. One of the two disputants, Fancy, is immediately pleased with the idea, but still has an objection that appears to spring from vanity. Reason responds more slowly, but when she gives her judgment, Fancy moderates her pride, and all parts of the Mind together receive much more pleasure than had originally been envisaged from the suggestion of Fancy alone.

1 *appallèd*: enfeebled, staled

3 *argued books diffuse*: OED does not record an adjectival use of 'argued'; 'diffuse' could have the modern meaning of 'excessively wordy,' but more probably has the obsolete sense of 'confused,'

'obscure.' Blundeston's compressed phrase suggests that his mind is exhausted by reading weighty tomes of minutely reasoned argument – perhaps by Sidney's philosopher, who 'setting down with thorny argument the bare rule, is so hard of utterance and so misty to be conceived, that one that hath no other guide but him shall wade in him till he be old before he shall have sufficient reason to be honest' (*Apology* 106–7).

7 *humours*: vapours, fluids

12 *fieldish*: of the fields; not recorded in this sense in OED.

22 *Pentecost*: or Whitsun, the seventh Sunday after Easter; the major Christian feastday gathered to itself midsummer celebrations, and was a major holiday and festival period. Shakespeare's Julia in *The Two Gentlemen of Verona* passed the time in 'pageants of delight' (IV ii 164), and Perdita at a later season recalls the playfulness of 'Whitsun pastorals' (*The Winter's Tale* IV iv 134).

25 *Quod*: quoth, said

25 *brake*: broke off

26 *Bayard*: See 'As bold as blind Bayard' (ODEP 72; Tilley B112). Bayard was the name of the horse given by Charlemagne to Renaud (Rinaldo), and also a common name for a bay-coloured horse. The origin was forgotten in proverbial sayings, and 'Bayard' came to be taken as the type of blindness or blind recklessness (see OED, and Rowland 127–8).

31 *clew*: a ball of thread: Blundeston's reference is to the secret hiding place of the labyrinth, which needed a guiding thread or clue to be safely discovered.

42 *filèd*: polished

42 *flowing head*: fertile brain; the phrase suggests a smooth and graceful style, and also eloquent copiousness.

46 *Pyrenei*: 'Mountains, which do divide France from Spain' (Cooper)

49 *truss*: bundle, pack

64 *Aesop's crow*: The bird who foolishly sought to beautify himself with the feathers of others (usually the peacock) is variously named, but usually in Latin is *cornix*, or crow. In William Powell's 1551 edition of Aesop's fables, the title explains 'how none ought to be proud of other men's gear' (lxxiii).

76 *sappy*: full of goodness or substance. This line is the first example of the sense cited by OED.

88 *wrest herself*: dispose or incline herself; see OED *v* †3, though no reflexive usage is exemplified.

88 *quite*: make a return for, repay

93–4 *Who absent ... whatsoever faileth him*: The poems will commend Googe and make up whatever may be lacking to him in his absence.

WOODCUT See Textual Appendix pp 198–9.

Daphnes, Amintas: The names of the speakers in the first eclogue have been added to the factotum woodcut. The names of Googe's shepherds come from common pastoral stock. Most of them are to be found in Virgil's eclogues (Daphnes, Amintas, Dametas, Tityrus, Menalcas, Coridon, Alexis, Melibeus, Palemon, Mopsus, Egon, Coridon); Googe probably derives Faustus and Cornix from Mantuan; Felix, Silvanus, Syrenus, Selvagia and Diana from Montemayor. On generic names in pastoral literature see Alastair Fowler 77–82.

5 Egloga prima.

Googe's examination of the hazards of passionate love is initiated when the young shepherd Daphnes asks the elderly Amintas for a tale. Amintas responds with a lengthy definition of sensual love. Despite the passion's manifold pains, he concludes that lawfully sanctioned heterosexual love is still better than Jove's wicked passion for Ganymede. Daphnes seems suitably grateful for the old shepherd's exposition, and acknowledges his almost parental authority by giving him in thanks a whistle that had belonged to his father. In discussing the sources of this eclogue, Peirce notes parallels in situation and pastoral trappings with Mantuan's first eclogue (in the request to tell a tale of antique loves), his third (in the time of the year), and his eighth (in the reference to the sign of the Ram); he also suggests the name Amintas may refer to either of Mantuan's characters of the same name (in the second, third, and sixth eclogues). Peirce argues that Googe's general discussion of the power of love parallels and verbally echoes Hoby's translation of Castiglione's *Courtier*. His suggestion that Googe's 'platonism' may derive from Ficino's commentary on the *Symposium* is less convincing (235–45).

1 *Phoebus*: 'Apollo, the son of Jupiter and Latona, and is taken for the sun' (Cooper).

8 *right equinoctial line*: Googe is apparently describing the vernal equinox, 'one of the two points at which the sun's path crosses the Equator, described technically as the first points in Aries and Libra' (OED). The date indicated is 20 March. The astrological opening is more suggestive of the native English poetic tradition, for example

the beginning of *The Canterbury Tales*, than of the Latin eclogue, whether Virgilian or Mantuanesque. Googe may also have been influenced here by Palingenius.

9 *Whereas*: where. 'Whereas,' 'whenas,' and 'whileas' for 'where,' 'when,' and 'while,' printed as one word or two, are common in Googe's poetry, perhaps because of their usefulness in achieving metrical regularity.

9 *the Ram*: Aries

11 *spoiled*: despoiled, deprived

15 *stayed*: supported, given occasion for. Tales for winter nights are here seen as rustic, but not necessarily trivial or idle. The tale that Aeneas sees as apt for winter in Marlowe's *Dido* (III iii 59) is his meeting with Venus: a momentous event subjected to much moralizing in Renaissance literature.

19 *sagèd*: befitting a sage; characterized by wisdom. This is a nonce-word; its usage here and at 31 provide the only examples in OED.

53 *Cupid, king of fiery love*: Compare Palingenius: 'O Lord, what rage of flames, and fire in every place to reign / This boy hath caused?' (48).

53–60 Peirce (237–8) compares this passage with Castiglione *The Courtier*, 'And because I know my selfe unworthie to talke of the most holy mysteries of love, I beseech him to leade my thought and my tongue so, that I may shew this excellent Courtier how to love contrary to the wonted manner of the common ignorant sorte' (312).

65–84 Peirce (238–9) compares Castiglione *The Courtier*, 'For those lively spirits that issue out at the eyes, because they are engendred nigh the hart, entring in like case into the eyes that they are levelled at, like a shaft to the pricke, naturally pearce to the hart ... and with the most subtill and fine nature of bloud which they carrie with them, infect the bloude about the hart ... Wherefore by litle and litle ... these messengers kindle with the puffing of desire the fire that so burneth ...' (247; see also 316, 312–13). See also Surrey's 'The Lover describes his restless state' (Tottel no 24) and Wyatt's 'The Lover describeth his being taken with the sight of his Love' (Tottel no 89).

73 *Plato*: The reference appears to be to *Phaedrus*, where love is a sickness or disease or malady (231), a madness (244), and a kind of fever caught from the effects of beauty entering the eyes (251, and also 253 and 255).

85–100 Peirce (242) compares Castiglione *The Courtier*, 'deceived ... they forthwith returne again to unbridled coveting, and with the very same trouble which they felt at the first, they fall againe into the raging and most burning thirst of the thing, that they hope in vaine to possesse perfectly ... both in the beginning and middle of this love, there is never other thing felt, but afflictions, torments, griefes, pining travaile, so that to be wan, vexed with continuall teares and sighes, to live with a discontented minde, to be alwaies dumbe, or to lament, to covet death ...' (305).

87 *seely*: pitiable, helpless

103–16 Peirce (243–4) compares Castiglione *The Courtier*, 'Whereupon the poares be dried up and withered, and yet doth the remembrance of beautie somewhat stirre those vertues of the soule in such wise, that they seeke to scatter abroade the spirits, and they finding the wayes closed up, have no issue, and still they seeke to get out, and so with those shootings inclosed, pricke the soule, and torment her bitterly ... And hence come the teares, sighes, vexations and torments of lovers: because the soule is alwaies in affliction and travell and (in a manner) waxeth woode, until the beloved beautie commeth before her once againe, and then she is immediately pacified and taketh breath ...' (316–17).

117–20, 125–32 Peirce (245) compares Ovid *Remedia amoris* 725–6, 729–30.

151–2 *wicked love ... in Ganymede's time*: Ganymede (here pronounced with four syllables) was 'the son of Tros, king of Phrygia, a boy of passing beauty and feminine countenance, taken up into the skies by an eagle at Jupiter's commandment, and made his butler' (Googe 'A Table'). See Ovid's *Metamorphoses* x 152–61. Lemprière comments: 'Some say he was carried away by an eagle, to satisfy the shameful and unnatural desires of Jupiter' (250). See also Palingenius: 'Use not the love of boys, take heed, such love is sinful shame' (16).

161 *Fetch in the goat*: Peirce (236) compares Mantuan's first eclogue 175–6.

169–73 Peirce (236) suggests the gift of the whistle may derive from Virgil's fifth eclogue 81–90.

6 Egloga secunda.

Dametas's suicidal lament over his hopeless love parallels Virgil's second eclogue, where Coridon laments Alexis's indifference (one of the gifts by which Corydon hopes to woo Alexis is a pipe bequeathed to him by Damoetas on his deathbed). Googe appears to be suggesting that misplaced and excessive heterosexual love has just as dire consequences as the 'wicked love' condemned in the preceding eclogue. Peirce notes: 'It is quite possible that the idea of this eclogue was suggested by the theme of unlawful love in Mantuan's second and third, and the plight of Dametas is not unlike that of Mantuan's unhappy Amyntas. Both die as a result of excessive passion' (250). However, he prefers to tie the poem to the native English tradition, to ballads, and to such poems as Tottel no 181, 'Harpelus complaynt of Phillidaes love bestowed on Corin, who loved her not and denied him, that loved her' (251–2). Panofsky sees this poem as 'a simplified deliberative oration'; 'the argument has two stages, an exposition of facts and then a discussion of possible responses to the facts.' He compares it with Marvell's 'To his Coy Mistress,' concluding that 'Googe seeks a collection of strong thematic images, not a complex texture or an intricacy of argument' (167–8). He also compares it with Sidney's 'Go my flocke' (*Astrophil and Stella*, Ninth Song), and with two anonymous poems in *The Gorgeous Gallery of Gallant Inventions* (168–75).

3–4 *fear'st thou ... to die*: Compare Ovid *Heroides* IX 146 (Deianira to Hercules), repeated at 152, 158, 164: *impia quid dubitas Deianira mori*? ('O wicked Deianira, why hesitate to die'). Googe's use of a refrain may also have been influenced by Virgil's eighth eclogue.

7 *flood*: river

17 *sith*: since

47 *addict*: to devote oneself habitually. The first recorded use is 1577 *OED* (4b). See Rubel 134.

51–2 *plough ... sands*: a variant of the proverbial expressions of sowing or ploughing the sands, much used by poets (*ODEP* 757, 635; Tilley s87, s89). See Ovid *Heroides* v 115–16. The mention of rocks may have been influenced by *Heroides* x 132, when Ariadne accuses Theseus 'they who begot you were the rocks and the deep!'

57 *brutish*: animal as opposed to human; the word readily takes on a pejorative sense of the savage or irrational, but that does not seem to be the intention here (cf 13.1).

7 Egloga tertia.

The opening conversation about the ousting of Coridon's ram by Dametas's continues from the last eclogue the theme of the woe of passionate desire, relating it more obviously to animal nature. The shepherds turn to considering *the town's estate* (53). Modern urban vices are condemned by contrasting by-gone virtues; particularly lamentable is the passing of true nobility. General criticism becomes particular satirical allegory with the introduction of the Coridon *come from the cart* (113), and references to contemporary religious problems. The shepherds comfort themselves with the thought that the vices of the town will provoke God's scourge and plague, and the eclogue ends with a reminder of contented pastoral lowliness in the invitation to Coridon's cottage. Peirce finds in this eclogue a general resemblance to Mantuan's sixth, in the criticism of the town and the decision to stay in the country, but notes that the main themes of the two eclogues differ (260–1). The relationship between the two eclogues is closely examined by J.D. Alsop (1984), who stresses Googe's originality in the handling of his material, and points out that Googe's satire is directed at upstart rustics as well as at the *sinful sights* in *townish lands*.

1–8 Peirce compares the opening description of the weather with Mantuan's second eclogue 28–30, and the ailing ram with the goat in his fourth eclogue and the ram in his ninth (261–2).

48–65 Crinò cites line 48 in illustration of the bucolic convention also used by Spenser in his April eclogue 31. She also cites Googe's acclimatization of moral personifications to bucolic poetry in illustration of Spenser's February eclogue 87–90 (346, 341).

59 *abject*: an outcast or degraded person

79 *Sir John Straw ... Cur* contemptuously dismissive names for underbred upstarts. The use of Sir John as a contemptuous appellation for a priest (OED †3) may also be relevant.

80 *degenerate*: change in kind; show an alteration from normal type

83 *fish bred up*: proverbial; see Tilley F305.

97–100 *ODEP* 16; Tilley A262–3. Taverner, translating Erasmus, notes 'This proverb advertiseth us that the ornaments of fortune do not change the nature of man ... It is to be feared lest at this day there be in Christendom many apes (that is to say counterfeiters which by a Greek word we commonly call hypocrites) decked in purple badges and cognizances, that is to wit, which bear outward signs and badges of great holiness as though they were lambs, but inwardly they be ravening wolves' (*Proverbes or Adagies* [1539] C5–6).

102 *masty*: mastiff

106 *in field*: on the battlefield

107 *chop*: change, alteration; not recorded in quite this form in OED: *sb*[3] 1 gives the definition 'An exchange, a barter,' and records one example from *a*1670, and 2 gives 'Chop and change,' with the first example from 1759. The verb meaning 'to barter or sell' and the verbal phrase 'to chop and change' were both current in the sixteenth century.

109–28 The identity of the two Coridons has caused some debate. The evil neatherd is tentatively identified by Frank Fieler (xiii) as Stephen Gardiner, Bishop of Winchester, and Lord Chancellor of England in Mary's reign. However, Timothy Cook argues that the two Coridons must refer to two of Googe's acquaintance of the same name, and argues for Barnabe Rich the author, and 'the notorious Richard Rich, Lord Chancellor of England from 1548–1551' (497–9). Alsop provides various other candidates: his prime suspect for villain is Stephen Gardiner, partnered by George Gardiner, who was at Cambridge while Googe was there and who later became Dean of Norwich and chaplain to Queen Elizabeth, as the good shepherd Coridon. Alsop also advances arguments for Edmund Bonner, Bishop of London, Nicholas Heath, Archbishop of York, and Thomas Watson, Bishop of Lincoln as possible churlish Coridons (512–16). The case for Stephen Gardiner seems strongest, partly because of the connection with Googe's family (see Introduction p 5). Alsop's difficulties with date of composition seem unnecessary in light of the ability Googe shows in the epitaphs on Sheffield and Shelley to respond with animation to events in the past.

115–16 *governs us. Because ... wit,*: The punctuation of the 1563 text attaches the clause to the preceding sentence: 'governs us: because ... wit.'

119 *seely*: innocent, harmless

133–6 Presumably a reference to the Marian exiles.

137–44 *Daphnes ... Alexis*: The favoured candidates for the leading Protestants veiled under these names are any two of Cranmer, Latimer, and Ridley. Cranmer, as *the chiefest*, seems to have some claim to be Daphnes, but *There* might also suggest that Daphnes died in exile, rather than in the fires of St Giles. J.D. Alsop is probably right in his assertion that the identity of Daphnes and Alexis, like that of the two Coridons, cannot be determined with certainty (see note to 109–28 above).

152 *townish*: pertaining to the town; also characteristic of town life

163–4 *a stormy shower*: Peirce (262) compares Mantuan's second eclogue 172–3 and third eclogue 192–3.

165–72 Peirce (262–3) compares Virgil's first eclogue 79–83, and Mantuan's ninth 14–16.

8 Egloga quarta.

The sensational subject matter of the fourth eclogue, in which the spirit of Dametas returns from hell to warn against foolish love, is matched by the abrupt and dramatic form of Melibeus's emotional apostrophe and narration. The opening apostrophe gives a strongly moral and religious cast to the warning against love. Peirce comments: 'Connected with the religious theme, and related to the medieval narrative tradition, is the use in pastoral poetry of the vision. In one of Boccaccio's eclogues the poet's dead daughter appears to describe the life hereafter; in Mantuan Pollux is converted after seeing a lovely lady. Googe uses the same device in Eclogue IV, but his purpose is to have Dametas utter a Jeremiad against the dangers of earthly love' (228). He notes that Googe's main models for such ghostly visitations were *The Mirror for Magistrates* and Seneca's tragedies (271); that 'Mantuan's second and third eclogues may have suggested the theme of unlawful love; and Mantuan's fourth, the satire on women' (272); and that the poem 'Of a lover that made his onely God of his love' (Tottel no 226) provides a particularly interesting parallel because of similarities in phrasing (273).

1–8 Compare Palingenius: 'The king, and Lord, and mighty power, that rules the world so vast: / Who with a beck the golden stars, shall govern whilst they last' (9). Googe may also be referring to the first and perfect world held in the mind of God (see *Batman uppon Bartholome* VIII i), discussed by Palingenius in 'Libra': 'This same first framèd world … / In which the chiefest life is God, where Saints as Stars appear, / And therefore stranger things are there, than are perceived here' (118).

9–20 The apparition of a ghost to recount its own dismal tale had recently been popularized by *The Mirror for Magistrates* (1559).

31–2 *Magaera … Tisiphon … Alecto*: the Furies, or Eumenides. Googe has separate entries for the first two in the 'Table' to Palingenius (1561), each being described as 'one of the furies in hell.'

47 *Deiopey*: Googe may have borrowed the name of the fatal beauty from Virgil's *Aeneid* I 72, where this most beautiful of Juno's nymphs is offered to Aeolus by the queen of the gods as a reward for his harassment of Aeneas on his journey to Italy.

83 *bridle to my will*: To give a horse the bridle is to abandon control of him.

91–5 *A creature … a woman*: This brief excursion on a familiar theme is probably most directly prompted by Mantuan's enthusiastically lengthy diatribe Egloga IV 110–245 (translated by Turbervile [1567] F1v–F8v).

94 *pilled*: beggarly, meagre (*OED* †3 †b fig): 'a miserable example of pride'

95 *mate*: the sense of either 'companion' or 'one of a wedded pair' would be apt (OED 1 †c and 3a): in either case Googe is evidently using the word contemptuously or satirically.
98 *an ugly fiend*: Compare the 'ugly feend' who stalks Guyon in the Cave of Mammon (FQ II vii 26–7). The function of Googe's fiend also suggests Charon, whose horrendous aspect is described by Virgil at *Aeneid* VI 298–301.
108 *wood*: ferocious
115–20 These lines seem a conscious contradiction of the final lines of Surrey's 'Complaint of a dying lover' (Tottel no 18), who is entombed beside Troilus by the shepherd who listened to his complaint, and 'Whose soule, by Angels power, departed not so sone, / But to the heavens, lo it fled, for to receive his dome.'
117 *Charon*: 'An old deformed knave, whom the Poets feigned to be ferryman of the rivers in hell' (Googe, 'A Table').

9 Egloga quinta.
The fifth eclogue introduces another catastrophe of love, this time of a woman destroyed by passion. The story of Claudia, Valerius, and Faustus is compressed, with some alterations, from Montemayor's *Diana* Book II, where the Lady Felismena, disguising herself as a boy, leaves the Court to follow her lover Don Felix, who has fallen in love with Celia (the story is most familiar from Shakespeare's use of it in *The Two Gentlemen of Verona*). Valerius is the name taken by Felismena, but Googe does not suggest that his Valerius is a woman in love with her master. Montemayor's Celia dies mysteriously during the night, whereas Claudia more dramatically stabs herself, like Seneca's Phaedra in *Hippolytus*. It is possible that Googe knew some of the many other versions of this story (see Kennedy in *Diana* pp l–li), but he is clearly working from Montemayor, and especially in Claudia's speech to Valerius translates closely (compare *Diana* p 102, ll 2–20). The focus is not, as in Montemayor, on Valerius / Felismena, but on Claudia's 'desperate act of love,' which in terms of Googe's design balances Dametas's catastrophe.
11 *Destinies*: the Fates, or Parcae; the three goddesses supposed to determine the course of human life.
17 *this Court*: An unexplained reminiscence of Montemayor's story, where there is considerable emphasis on the court of 'the great Princesse' and its 'store of blazing beauties, and gallant Ladies' (*Diana* p 87 l 6, p 91 l 20; Lopez Estrada p 104 ll 18–19, p 110 ll 22–27).
51 *astonied*: bewildered, dismayed

81 The irregular line of twelve syllables may indicate Claudia's passion, but is more probably a sign of haste in Googe's composition.
109 *the Princess*: In Montemayor, the death of Celia 'stroke all the court with no smal woonder' (*Diana* p 103 ll 1–2; Lopez Estrada p 124 ll 21–2).

10 Egloga sexta.

The sixth eclogue presents a man who, though grief-stricken, has survived the unhappy experience of love. His friend reproves his *fancy fond*, and through moral exhortation and appeals to the facts (*Since she is gone, what remedy*? 57), persuades him to listen to remedies for love. The names of Felix and Faustus appear to connect this with the preceding eclogue, and with *Diana* (Googe's Faustus in the fifth eclogue is Montemayor's Felix). T.P. Harrison feels that Faustus is the same character, and is lamenting his treatment of his former love (Valerius / Felismena), a part of Montemayor's story that Googe has not used in the fifth eclogue (73–4). However, the Faustus of the sixth eclogue is lamenting the loss of a beloved who is still alive, as 41–60 make clear. If there is a parallel with *Diana*, it is with the situation at the beginning of the pastoral romance, where Sylvanus attempts to comfort Syrenus for his loss of Diana through her marriage to Delius. Whatever connections it may have with Montemayor's romance, this eclogue depends most heavily on Ovid's *Remedia amoris*, a debt analysed at length by Peirce (286–93).
3 *holts*: wooded hills
8 *befall*: This unusual truncated form of the regular past participle 'befallen,' is evidently used for the sake of the rhyme.
11 *besprent*: besprinkled. Crinò cites 11–12 in illustration of Spenser's mourning muse 'with teares besprint' in his November eclogue 111 (365).
14 *willow*: The willow as a symbol of grief for unrequited or lost love is most familiar from Shakespeare's Dido (*The Merchant of Venice* v i 10) and Desdemona (*Othello* IV iii 30–59). See ODEP 874; Tilley W403.
42–4 *A Marigold*: a popular flower. There is another poetic description of its qualities, probably by Googe, in *The Overthrow of the Gout* (1577) (Schuler 79). Shakespeare refers frequently to it (*The Winter's Tale* IV iv 105–6; *Sonnet* 25; *The Rape of Lucrece* 397–9). Googe may have known the pious interpretation of it in Paradin's *Heroicall Devises* (as translated by P.S. in 1591: 'Margaret Queen of Navarre used a

most solemn sign, namely the marigold, whose colour resembleth so near the colour of the sun, as almost nothing more. For what way soever the sun goeth, it followeth it ... This godly Queen chose this kind of symbol, that she might evidently express, how that she referred all her cogitations, affections, vows, words and deeds to almighty God, only wise and everlasting, as one that meditated on heavenly things with all her heart' (c7v–8)).

70 *the blinded God*: Cupid. See E. Panofsky, 'Blind Cupid,' in *Studies in Iconology*; and also *Diana*: 'And it is so unruly, that it resultes oftentimes to the hurt and prejudice of the lover: since true lovers for the most part fall to hate and neglect themselves, which is not only contrary to reason, but also to the law of nature. And this is the cause why they paint him blinde, and void of all reason' (p 156 l 38–p 157 l 3).

77–80 *Leave off ... stray*: See Ovid *Remedia amoris* 79–80, 91, 117–18.

81–8 *The tender twig ... fervent fire*: See Ovid *Remedia amoris* 85–8, 117–20.

91 *thy festering wound*: Compare Ovid *Remedia amoris* 109–34.

93 *idleness*: See Ovid *Remedia amoris* 136–40, and Googe's 'To Alexander Neville,' numbered 29 in this edition.

97–108 See Ovid *Remedia amoris* 169–98.

103 *Scylla*: not one of the Scyllas of myth and legend (see note to 44.10), but a shepherdess

117 This line lacks two syllables.

122 *passèd*: cared

125–6 Crinò cites these lines in illustration of Spenser's 'pensife boy' in the January eclogue (338).

129 *infective*: infectious

137–72 See Ovid *Remedia amoris* 199–212: among other ways of shedding the otium or leisure that breeds love, Ovid recommends various kinds of hunting, including netting and snaring birds.

145 *shepstare*: starling: 'the name is said to refer to the bird's habit of perching on the backs of sheep to feed on the ticks' (OED, which cites this as the first example).

145–56 Googe may be taking this description of catching starlings from a poem he might have encountered in his travels to Spain, the second eclogue of Garcilaso de la Vega: when August heats are passed,

> Black clouds of starlings circle to and fro:
> Mark now the craft that we employed to snare

These birds that go through unobstructed air.
One straggler first from their vast companies,
Alive we captured, which was done with ease;
Next, to its foot a long limed thread we tied,
And when the passing squadron we descried,
Aloft we tossed it; instantly it mixed
Amongst the rest, and our success was fixed;
For soon, as many as the tangling string,
Or by the head, or leg, or neck, or wing,
In its aerial voyage twined around,
Flagged in their strength, and fell towards the ground (204–5).

The context of this possible borrowing is quite different from Googe: in Silva I of Garcilaso's second eclogue, Albanio is lamenting that he has lost his beloved through rashly declaring his love, and is at this point rehearsing to his friend the joys he and his beloved had shared in their youthful innocence. Here the delights of hunting and bird-snaring contribute to the growth of passionate love, rather than providing salutary distraction from it.

179 *Calisto*: or Callisto, the constellation of the bear. Calisto, a nymph of Diana, was seduced by Jupiter and changed into a bear by the jealous Juno. See Ovid *Metamorphoses* II 409–507.

181 *Cepheus ... with twining serpent*: King of Ethiopia, father of Andromeda by Cassiopeia, and one of the Argonauts, at his death Cepheus was changed into the northern constellation bearing his name, between Cassiopeia and Draco, or the dragon.

11 Egloga septima.

In the seventh eclogue all three of the speakers, two men and a woman, are suffering from unrequited or lost love. Both Syrenus and Selvagia have reason to complain of the inconstancy of their former loves, which gives rise to debate about the relative merits of the sexes. The style of the eclogue is easy and colloquial, with many abbreviated forms and elisions giving a lively tone of the speaking voice. Its substance is drawn from Book I of Montemayor's *Diana*, mainly from p 17 l 18 to p 32 l 6 (in Lopez Estrada p 19 l 8 to p 39 l 18). Following is a more detailed comparison of Googe's poem with *Diana* as translated by Yong:

1–20 cf *Diana* p 17 ll 18–35;
21–36 cf *Diana* p 18 ll 3–13;
37–44 are rather Googe's comment on Sirenus's behaviour than

translation, and are a substitute for the rest of Sirenus's speech in praise of his beloved, *Diana* p 18 ll 13–28;

45–64 owe something to *Diana* pp 21–4, especially p 24 ll 11–19;

66–80 cf *Diana* p 23 l 38–p 24 l 8;

81–94 cf *Diana* p 25 ll 25–34;

95–6 present Googe's own sententious and sardonic clinching comment;

97–120 are drawn from *Diana* p 28 l 25 to p 30 l 8, but are mainly Googe's own summary and transition rather than direct translation;

121–32 cf *Diana* p 30 ll 9–15;

133–6 cf *Diana* p 30 l 37–40;

137–44 Googe's addition;

145–60 cf *Diana* p 31 ll 11–21;

161–88 cf *Diana* p 31 ll 23–39;

189–92 cf *Diana* p 31 ll 21–3;

193–6 Googe's addition;

197–208 cf *Diana* p 32 ll 6–15, p 49 ll 3–4.

Silvanus's report of Diana's protestations of grief and constancy (54–64) may also be coloured by Cynthia's narrative song in Book II (*Diana* pp 60–74). Her behaviour is also reminiscent of Chaucer's Criseyde: (see *Troilus and Criseyde* v 689–700, IV 1534–54).

17 This line has two extra syllables, the first of several irregularities in versification in this eclogue, arising perhaps because Googe is so closely following his prose source. See also 23, 57, and 65 (all of which lack two syllables); and 91, in which the extra syllable cannot be swallowed by elision, though the line could be regularized by dropping *in*.

91 *quoiting*: playing the game of quoits. In 91–2 Googe is translating 'taner, cantar, luchar, jugar al cayado, baylar con las mocas el domingo' (Lopez Estrada p 30 ll 10–11), which Yong accurately translates 'piping, singing, wrestling, darting of our sheephookes, and dauncing with the wenches on Sunday' (*Diana* p 25 ll 31–3).

93 *he is*: Read he's: the first of a number of contractions of pronoun or noun and verb in this eclogue (see Introduction p 27).

95–6 Googe is balancing two proverbial sayings: 'Manners maketh man,' and 'Money makes the man' (in Latin, *Divitiae* rather than *Pecunia*). See ODEP 508, 539; Tilley M629, M1076.

114 *good-den*: good even, good evening

122 *women speeds*: See note to 3.3.

124, 150 *unconstant, unconstancy*: inconstant, inconstancy (obsolete)

125 *earnestliest*: most earnestly; not recorded in OED. Yong's 'you are so ready for the lightest thing in the worlde to forget them, to whom you have borne the greatest love' accurately translates the passage that Googe is freely paraphrasing (*Diana* p 30 ll 12–14).
143 *noughty*: bad, immoral
179 *chattering pies*: This proverbial image of the talkative magpie is added to the Spanish by Googe. For the proverbial expressions, see Whiting P179; Tilley P285.
180 *tongues must always walk*: Rubel compares Googe's use of this 'arresting metaphor' with Spenser *FQ* II iv 5 and Sidney *Astrophil and Stella* Eighth Song (244, 205).
195–6 *women must ... nay*: Googe's proverbial addition to the Spanish. See ODEP 911, Tilley W722.

12 Egloga octava.
The carefree pastoral life is now presented in a fully religious light. The contrast between the good and the wicked man is drawn in biblical terms, and the narrative then moves to an allegory of the foolishly wicked man's life and death, in the late medieval manner of *The Ship of Fools* and Skelton's *The Bouge of Court*. The closing pastoral scene is more lengthily developed than in earlier eclogues, the last image being of the unruly bull, reminding the reader of the need to control animal passions. Peirce sees in this eclogue the influence of Palingenius, and of 'several of Mantuan's eclogues, especially the seventh and eighth.' (306).
1–10 Peirce compares Mantuan's eighth eclogue 1–3 (306). Compare also Palingenius: 'the heat / When as the Sun doth fervent flame amid the Lion great: / Or when the raging Dog the fields, of green doth quite defeat' (14).
1 *Titan*: 'The brother of Saturn, and is taken for the Sun' (Cooper)
5 *fiery Dog*: a constellation. OED cites Googe's translation of Heresbach's *Husbandry*: 'The great heat of the Sun ... is most extreme at the rising of the lesser Dog.'
8 *misers*: miserable wretches
24–144 These lines are deeply imbued with biblical ideas and phrases, with the Psalms being the strongest influence. For God as king, creator, and overlooker of the deeds of men, see particularly Psalms 24, 84, 95, 33, 103, 104. For the contrasted fates of good and evil men, see for example Psalms 36 and 37. For the folly of those who ignore God, see Psalms 14 and 53.
55–6 *angels ... attends*: Compare Psalm 91:11–12.

65 *misers*: Wretches, but with some sense of those who are niggardly in returning God's love
73–84 Compare Psalms 112 and 119.
85–8 Compare Psalm 34:7.
89–90 *the Prophet ... Daniel*: Daniel 6:16–23. The 1563 edition identifies the prophet as David. The slip may be the compositor's rather than Googe's.
91–2 *Moses*: Exodus 2:11
92 *seely*: innocent, harmless
93–4 *Elias*: or Elijah, 1 Kings 17:2–8
99–100 *Jupiter / ... embracing boys*: See note to 5.150, and Ovid *Metamorphoses* X 152–219.
103–4 *Saturn*: 'The son of heaven and earth: who begat of his own sister, Jupiter, Juno, Neptune, and Pluto' (Googe 'A Table'). The malice and melancholy of Saturn are perhaps most familiar to modern readers through Chaucer's *Knight's Tale*; see also E. Panofsky, especially 76–9.
107–8 *Venus /Cupido*: One of Stephen Batman's additions to his 1582 edition of Bartholomaeus's encyclopedia *De proprietatibus rerum* identifies Venus thus: 'the Goddess of lasciviousness and wanton lust: by the which is signified uncleanly copulation, she came of the kindred from Saturn. Lo, of what antiquity is whoredom among the Pagan Gentiles, and still maintained of those, that should be Christians, specially forbidden by God in the 20. of Exodus' (*Batman uppon Bartholome* VIII 26).
126–7 *merciful ... revenging slow*: Compare Exodus 34:6–7; Numbers 14:18; Psalm 103:8.
132 *turns away His face*: Compare 2 Chronicles 6:42, 30:9.
134–44 *How long*: Compare Numbers 14:11–12.
152–8 Rosemond Tuve criticizes this passage as an insufficiently developed *allegoria* (*Elizabethan and Metaphysical Imagery* 107–8). She is kinder to Googe's concept of Excess in *Cupido Conquered* 600–16.
154 *hoises*: hoists
174 *mate*: rival, vie with, with a pun on the chess usage, checkmate
174 *a Nec in hemp*: OED gives Nec as an obsolete form of Neck, which is clearly the primary meaning here. Also, a neck in chess is a move to cover check. There may also be a reference to the Latin negative. However, the 1563 text treats the word like a proper name. There may be, then, an allusion to an individual whose arrogant pretensions will be negated, and who may end up with his neck in a rope

for daring to checkmate a knight. Surrey's poem built on a chess figure may have suggested to Googe his more complex allusion: 'Although I have a checke / To geve the mate is harde / For I have found a necke / To keepe my Men in garde' ('To the Ladie that skorned her Lover,' Tottel no 21).

177–88 Cornix does not acknowledge Coridon's interjection, but continues the imagined speech of the 'brainless fool.'

192 *the smarting rod*: See, for example, Psalm 89:32; Proverbs 10:13, 26:3.

197 *death* (*that old devouring wolf*): Compare 'the wulf the devyll devourer of mannes soule' (cited OED *sb* 4). For Shakespeare the wolf is the sentinel of 'wither'd murder' (*Macbeth* II i 52–3). See also Rowland, especially 104, 108–10.

215–20 *wretched man … seas of sin*: quoted by ODEP 795 as first illustration of the proverb Who swims in sin shall sink in sorrow

226 *sin-drowned*: OED notes that combinations such as this (sin-born, sin-crushed, etc) 'are extremely common from about 1590 to 1670, and again from about 1850.' Googe's usage, the first cited in OED, anticipates the fashion by thirty years.

242 *Phoebus*: Peirce compares Mantuan's third eclogue 192–3 (306–7).

247 *heronshew*: heron: also spelt heronsew, and suggested as an emendation for the handsaw that Hamlet claimed to have no difficulty distinguishing a hawk from (*Hamlet* II ii 367).

253–6 Peirce compares Mantuan's fourth eclogue, 89–90 (306n).

13 An Epitaph of the Lord Sheffield's death.

Edmund Sheffield, first Baron Sheffield (1521–49), was killed during Kett's rebellion in Norwich in August 1549 (see DNB 18:16). He had accompanied Northampton to suppress the rising, but his death contributed to a reverse for the King's forces. The rebels were finally put down by a force under Warwick. Archbishop Parker, who had played a part in attempting to talk the rebels into conformity, later encouraged Alexander Neville to write a Latin account of the uprising, which was published in 1575. The following is Neville's account of Sheffield's death, in the very close translation of R. Woods (1615):

> But the miserable death of the Lord Sheffield was lamented and pitied of all men. Who (as it came to pass) while he was more mindful of his birth and dignity than of his safety, swift and fierce and desirous of performing the

work he had in hand, setting upon the thickest of the enemies, and fighting too boldly and carelessly, by chance in his swift course fell from his horse headlong into a ditch, where this noble man was most cruelly slain of a villainous murderer. And when he besought him and his company, by all means possible (as by promising great rewards, by signifying his nobility, and the account of his name) to spare his life: yet was it far off, that either the man, or his name, could move any compassion, as they grew the more cruel. And after, they contended among themselves for the glory and commendation of this villainy (seldom heard of) as of a most noble act. So all of them boiled in mind, as it came almost to blows, while on both sides the desire of commendation and vainglory carried them, which seemed to be due unto him, that gave that fatal and deadly wound unto this worthy noble man; but by the opinion of them all, Fulke carried away the praise, which openly protested (calling God to witness) that he gave him his deadly wound with his club (Giiiv).

Fulke is himself long not after 'paid home,' but the death of Sheffield is a turning point, heartening the rebels and contributing to the flight and dispersal of the army 'partly strucken with the death of this noble young gentleman' (Giiiir). Holinshed, who draws extensively on Neville's account, identifies the villain as 'a butcherly knave named Fulks, who by occupation was both a carpenter and a butcher' (3:974). After describing the rebellions of 1549, Holinshed gives in full as 'a necessary discourse for every good English subject' Sir John Cheke's *The hurt of sedition*, first printed anonymously in 1549 and reprinted in 1569 and 1576. This highly interesting statement of Tudor attitudes to religion, rebellion, and egalitarianism takes Sheffield's death as an exemplar of the ills following rebellion, 'whenas man's body being a part of the whole commonwealth is wrongfully touched any way, and specially by death, then suffereth the commonwealth great injury.' Cheke praises Sheffield as one 'loved of every man, and hated of no man,' and chides the rebels:

ye slew him cruelly, who offered himself manfully, nor would not so much spare him for ransom, who was worthy for nobleness to have had honour & hewed him bare whom ye could not hurt armed, and by slavery slew nobility, in deed miserably, in fashion cruelly, in cause devilishly. Oh with what cruel spite was violently sundered so noble a body from so godly a mind? (3:996)

The sense of outrage in Googe's poem evidently derives from the sense of order overturned by 'base and vile persons' who 'bitterly inveighed against the authority of Gentlemen, and of the Nobility' (Neville, tr Woods BIV). Such behaviour is 'ungodly' and contrary to all religious duty. (Compare Eclogue 3 for a similar equation of social chaos and religious disturbance.) This poem is also notable for the personal indignation expressed; Googe may, as Peterson suggests (139–41), be experimenting in the heroic style, and trying to give personal feeling by introducing his own name (a trick which Sheidley (1968) 139 suggests he learned from Grimald), but his emotions may have been aroused by his association in 1560/1 with Arthur Golding, whose brother-in-law the sixteenth Earl of Oxford was also brother-in-law to Sheffield. Rollins believes that Sheffield was among the contributors to Tottel's *Miscellany*, since 'a "book of sonnets" of his composition is mentioned by Bale, Thomas Fuller, and others' (Tottel 2:84). Panofsky sees this and the epitaph on Shelley as types of *encomium*: here Googe 'elaborates the pathos of a nobleman being slain by common soldiers but affirms his honor in dying for his country' (90–1).

3 *tanner's bond*: Although according to the DNB 11:76–7 Robert Kett and his brother William were landowners of an old family, at the time of the rebellion Robert was regularly called a tanner and his brother a butcher or mercer. Cheke plays sarcastically on the word in addressing the 'rabble of Norfolk rebels' who pretend a 'marvellous tanned commonwealth,' choosing 'to disobey your betters, and to obey your tanners, to change your obedience from a king to a Kett' (Holinshed 3:989).

7 *clubbish*: boorish, rude

7 *crabbèd*: Churlish, harsh

11 *masty*: mastiff

21 *boisterous*: massive, bulky. The first use recorded in OED is 1596. Rubel suggests that Turbervile 'borrowed this neologism from Googe' (172n).

21 *bill*: a shafted weapon with a hook and beak cutting head (compare the pruning tool, billhook). As Pinkerton notes, 'Here Googe has actually sacrificed historical truth for the sake of alliteration' (142). Shakespeare was probably not glancing directly at Googe when he described Pyramus' death: 'with blade, with bloody blameful blade, / He bravely broach'd his boiling bloody breast' (*A Midsummer Night's Dream* v i 145–6).

26 *Hector*: 'The most valiant of all the Trojans, and the terror of the

Grecians beseiging his country. For so long as he lived, Troy could never be taken' (Cooper).

27 *carlish*: churlish, vulgar, mean

31 *doggèd*: currish, cruel

14 An Epitaph of M. Shelley slain at Musselburgh.

Edward Shelley, a master of the household of Henry VIII, treasurer of the council of the north, and captain of Berwick, was killed on 10 September 1547 at the battle of Musselburgh (near Edinburgh), now usually referred to as the battle of Pinkie. (See DNB 18:41–2. DNB refers to 'Sir Edward,' but he is not so entitled by Patten or Chaloner.) As the poem relates, Shelley won fame for being first into battle. Grafton, in his *Chronicles* (1569), gives the situation clearly: among the 'noble men and other that were officers' he lists 'Edward Shelley, the Lord Grey's Lieutenant of the men of arms of Boulogne, who was the first that gave the onset, and died most honourably in the aforesaid battle' (5v3r); and he summarizes the situation at the beginning of the battle thus:

> For suddenly the Scots being encamped in a valley by the river of Esk, arose and made great haste up the hill, minding to have obtained the hill, the wind and the sun, which if they had gotten, then our men had been much hindered, the which thing the Englishmen perceived, who as then were not in good array, neither could their army of footmen come so soon to the recovery of the hill as they would. Wherefore to stop the Scots of their purpose, the Lord Grey being Captain of the horsemen, was forced (partly out of order) to set forward, and to give the onset upon the Scots, only to stay them from the hill. The which English Horsemen nobly and valiantly encountered the Scots footmen, but the Scots stood so close, and were so defended with their pikes, that our men could not enter. By reason whereof divers of the English gentlemen that gave the onset were overthrown and slain (5v2r–v).

Another circumstance that added to the difficulties of this first charge was that the opposing army was arrayed on a ploughed field, and the furrows lay athwart the course of the English horsemen.

The chief account of the battle is William Patten's *The expedition into Scotland ... set out by way of Diary*, printed by Grafton in January 1548 (quotations are from *Tudor Tracts 1532–1588*, ed A.F. Pollard, 3:51–155, which reprints the text from Edward Arber's *English Gar-*

ner [London 1880]. Patten, together with 'Master William Cecil,' was one of the judges of the Marshalsea, and in this capacity they both 'had liberty to ride to see the things that were done, and leisure to note occurrences that came.' Patten's account is partly dependent on notes supplied by Cecil (155). One of the most dramatic moments is the cry of triumph that greets the sounding of the Scots' retreat, followed by a description of the stripping of the dead bodies, working back 'even from as far as the chase went, unto the place of our onset.' Here they find 'our men so ruefully gashed and mangled, in the head especially, as not one could, by the face, be known who he was,' and there 'Edward Shelley, alas, that worthy gentleman and valiant Captain! lay all pitifully disfigured and mangled among them; and nothing discernable but by his beard.' At this point Patten pauses to lament 'my so near friend,' comparing him to Curtius and the two Decii, whose heroic stories are summarized in the margins of the text. He does not mean to derogate fame from others, 'but only to do that in me may lie, to make his name famous who, among these, in my opinion, towards his Prince and country, did best deserve' (129–31). Sir Thomas Chaloner, who took a prominent part in the battle and who was a close friend of Cecil's, also celebrated Shelley's heroism in a 552-line Latin poem printed with his other Latin verse and following his poem *De republica Anglorum* (published posthumously in 1579), in which he praises Shelley as an example of fortitude, and compares him with such heroes as Mutius, Curtius, and the two Decii. This poem is distinguished by being prefixed by a prose address of 'Nicolaus Philandreius' to the reader, which also praises Shelley for the heroic virtue of fortitude. (See also Peirce 66, 323–5.)

Patten's richly eloquent Preface gives an interesting context for this story of heroism: he chides the Scots for breaking faith, wondering what could make them 'so untruly to sever from the bonds both of promise and covenant as ye will needs provoke your friends to plain revengement of open war'; and assures them of the purity of English intentions: 'We covet not to keep you bound, that would so fain have you free, as well from the feigned friendship of France … as also from the most servile thraldom and bondage under that hideous monster, that venomous *aspis* and very *ANTICHRIST*, the Bishop of *ROME*.' This leads to a lengthy denunciation of 'this precious prelate' and all 'his trimtrams and gewgaws' (66–74).

Patriotism and religious fervour probably influenced Googe's choice of subject in this and the preceding epitaph, but it may be felt that he relies too heavily on the fame of his subjects to give substance to his treatment. As Peterson objects: 'The narratives provide only the barest details, at best only a sketch of their respective actions, with the consequence that the heroic convention is unsupported' (141). Panofsky regards this poem as an encomium that 'narrates a specific fatal incident so as to show the imitable marks of soldierly courage that the victim displayed' (91). Peirce compares the Latin epitaph by Sir Thomas Chaloner, *De Heroica Edoardi Schellaei nobilissimi iuvenis Britanni fortitudine*, published posthumously in 1579 at the end of *De republica Anglorum*, but possibly known to Googe before 1562 (323). See also the Introduction pp 12–13.

2 *fumish*: irascible, passionate

3 *Bellona*: goddess of war, variously supposed the sister, daughter, or wife of Mars

8, 12 *troth*: Googe is playing on the senses 'good faith, loyalty,' 'one's faith as pledged or plighted in a solemn agreement,' and 'a promise, covenant.'

12 *trothless*: faithless, perfidious, disloyal

13 *in battle brave*: *Battle* refers to a body of troops in battle array, here used of the entire army; *brave* is more probably intended in the sense of 'splendid' than 'courageous.'

18 *staves*: lances or pikes

31 *maidly*: resembling a maid (maiden). OED gives as examples only this line, and one other of 1565.

33 *Brutus*: See note to 43.2–4.

40 *ne*: nor; compare 16.12.

49 *chargèd staff*: lance levelled for the charge (see OED charge *v*21)

51 *swifty*: swift; according to OED, a rare word, chiefly poetical

15 An Epitaph of Master Thomas Phaer.

Phaer (c1510–August 1560) was educated at Oxford and Lincoln's Inn, and was notable as a lawyer and a physician, as well as for his accomplishments as poet and translator. He translated the first seven books of the *Aeneid* at various periods from May 1555 to December 1557, and published them in May 1558 with a dedication to Queen Mary. He completed the eighth book on 10 September 1558, and the ninth on 3 April 1560, but he was prevented from finishing the tenth by an injury that took away the use of his right hand, and eventually proved fatal. His friend William Wightman published all nine completed books with the surviving fragment of the tenth (up to line 286) in 1562, dedicating the volume to Sir Nicholas Bacon. At the end are printed two and a half lines from the tenth book (467–9), which Phaer translated the day before his death, and sent to Wightman 'subscribed with his left hand.' His translation was very highly regarded in the sixteenth century and, with the completion by Thomas Twyne (who evidently chose to ignore the last line of Googe's epitaph), was frequently reprinted up to 1620. Phaer was a close friend of George Ferrers, one of the most important contributors to the *Mirror for Magistrates*, and he himself contributed the story of Owen Glendower to the first edition of 1559. (See DNB 15:1026–7; Campbell 32f; Conley passim; Lewis 248–69.) With Googe's epitaph, Peirce compares Sir Thomas Chaloner's Latin *Epitaphium Thomae Phayri medici* published in *De republica Anglorum* (323); see above.

1 *Maro*: Virgil

5 *Parnassus*: 'A mountain in Greece, having two tops, under the which the nine Muses did inhabit or dwell' (Cooper)

8 *Minerva's brain*: Minerva was the 'goddess of wisdom and all good arts and sciences, born of Jupiter's brain without any mother ... By which devise poets give men to understand that the knowledge of all good arts and sciences, proceedeth not of man's wit, but out of the fountain of God's grace and wisdom' (Cooper).

11 *barren tongue*: For a survey of attitudes to English in the earlier Tudor period, see Jones, who quotes Googe and Phaer as early examples of confidence in the vernacular (170–1).

16 *each other poets*: For this use of 'each' where modern usage would expect 'all,' see Abbott 23.

17 *Henry Howard*: printed H. Hawarde in 1563, but the first name is clearly to be pronounced. The Earl of Surrey (1517–47), with Wyatt most famous of the courtly makers of Henry VIII's reign, and the leading poet of Tottel's *Songs and Sonnets*, is also famed in literary history for his blank verse translation of the *Aeneid* Books II and IV, also printed by Tottel in 1557.

18 *raught*: reached, achieved

21 *Grimald*: See below. His translation of Virgil is not known to have survived.

22 *Douglas*: Gavin Douglas (?1474–1522), third son of the fifth Earl of Angus, from 1515 Bishop of Dunkeld, completed his famed Scottish translation of the *Aeneid* in 1513. It circulated widely in manuscript, and in 1553 was printed in London by W. Copland, who 'carefully anglicized his copy, substituting English words and flexions and, as a staunch Protestant, permitting no "Popish" references to pass unaltered' (J.A.W. Bennett 85).

22 *won the ball*: The expression is not recorded in OED, OPED, Tilley, or Whiting. Googe uses it also in his translation of Palingenius: 'By luck in love the prince despised, the Clown [1561 and John] obtains the ball' (44).
27 *Apollo's beams*: the sun's beams
29 *envious Fates*: the Parcae, the three goddesses who presided over the birth and life of mankind
35 *unperfect*: imperfect, incomplete

16 An Epitaph of the Death of Nicholas Grimald.
Grimald was an outstanding humanist scholar, translator, dramatist, and poet. Born in 1519, he proceeded BA at Christ's College, Cambridge in 1539–40, BA at Merton College, Oxford in 1541–2, and MA in 1543–4. He was lecturer at Christ Church in 1547, and also had associations with Brasenose and Exeter Colleges. He probably knew Cecil at Cambridge, and in 1549 sent him from Oxford an account 'of the state of the University under the shadow of the Reformers, which shows that at this time he was a spy against Catholics' (Guiney 85). He was encouraged and admired by Bale, who arranged for the printing of Grimald's two important Latin plays, *Christus Redivivus* and *Archipropheta*, at Cologne in 1543 and 1548 respectively. In 1552 he was chaplain to Bishop Ridley, and when, under Mary, Ridley was imprisoned at Oxford, Grimald was imprisoned in the Marshalsea. In 1555 he recanted, or as Guiney has it 'with apparent suddenness embraced again the faith of his boyhood' (85). Despite the evidence marshalled by his twentieth-century biographer L.R. Merrill to demonstrate that he was a Judas who betrayed Latimer and Ridley to the stake (216–27), it seems most unlikely that Grimald would have retained the good opinion of such as Bale, Tottel, and Googe had he done anything worse than shift ground to avoid martyrdom – a not unfamiliar evasion in those changeable times. He was the third named contributor to Tottel's *Songs and Sonnets*, following Wyatt and Surrey, and shares with Surrey the honour of the first printed English blank verse. Warton's praise of his poetry is perhaps more truly just than the neglect and disparagement he has suffered in more recent times. Warton says that he 'yields to none of his contemporaries for a masterly choice of chaste expression, and the concise elegancies of didactic versification.' He praises the 'smartness' of his couplets as worthy of Pope, and recognizes his 'great quickness and variety of illustration,' bounded by 'good sense and propriety' (4:54–5). The date of his death is not known, but is usually given as before May 1562, on the basis of Googe's elegy and

Blundeston's address to the Reader. Guiney advances an attractive argument for a date early in 1559 (88–90). Panofsky regards this poem as a type of *encomium*, providing the opportunity for meditation and moral generalization (91–2). Peirce comments: 'The diction is comparable to that used by Nashe in his plague-song, or by Ralegh in his "Farewell to the Court"' (326).

In 1563 this poem is printed in alternate lines of 4 and 6 syllables, except lines 21 and 22, which are broken 5 and 5, perhaps to avoid breaking the words *doltish* and *witless*, but compare such word breaks as *la / bour* and *on / ly* in lines 2 and 17 of the next poem.

10 *gripe*: grasp, clutch; compare 22a. 21.

12 *Ne stays he at*: nor stops he at

17 *Muses*: 'The nine daughters of Jupiter and memory, ladies of learning' (Googe 'A Table'). Googe calls Calliope, the muse of eloquence and heroic poetry, 'the worthiest sister among the muses' (ibid).

18 *Minerva*: See note to 15.8.

25 *Fortune favours fools, as old men say*: proverbial: ODEP 281; Tilley F600. Stephens notes that old men means 'men of old; Googe uses a variation of this, "ancient men," in "The Uncertainty of Life"' (27).

17 To Master Alexander Nowell.

Nowell (?1507–1602) was (in the words of the DNB) 'a polished scholar, a weighty and successful preacher, a skilful disputant, and a learned theologian'; he was also a notable schoolmaster. He entered Brasenose College, Oxford in 1520, proceeded BA and was elected a fellow in 1526, proceeded MA in 1540, and in 1541 or 1542 gave public lectures. He took orders in 1543, and was appointed master of Westminster School. He was appointed a prebendary of Westminster in 1551. After the annulment of his election to Queen Mary's first parliament in 1553, he went abroad to escape the attentions of Bishop Bonner, first to Strasbourg and then to Frankfurt, 'where, being desirous of peace, he took a leading part in the attempt to compose the religious disputes of the exiles in 1557' (DNB 14:689). On Cecil's recommendation he was made archdeacon of Middlesex following his return from exile in 1559, and preached at the consecration of Edmund Grindal, Bishop of London (later Archbishop of Canterbury). Upon Queen Elizabeth's recommendation he was elected Dean of St Paul's in 1560. At Cecil's instigation he wrote in 1562–3 the *Catechism* for which he is chiefly remembered. He remained alert and active to the end of his long life – perhaps because of the fishing and ale-drinking that anecdotes in the *DNB* account indicate he enjoyed. His brother Lawrence, Dean of Lichfield, was a protégé of Cecil's, living at his house and tutoring the Earl of Oxford in 1563, and transcribing Anglo-Saxon and medieval manuscripts for both Cecil and Archbishop Parker (McKisack 53). Peirce comments on the use in this poem of the rhetorical figures *ecphonesis* at lines 7 and 9, *epizeuxis* and *metanoia* in 18, and *cacosyntheton* in 12 (329).

In 1563 this poem is printed in alternate lines of 4 and 6 syllables.

1 *Muses*: See note to 16.17.

4 *Phoebus*: 'Otherwise called Apollo, the god of eloquence and poetry' (Googe 'A Table')

4 *Minerva*: See note to 15.8.

12 *applied*: put to use, devoted to

18 To Doctor Bale.

Bale (1495–November 1563), theologian, book collector, literary historian, dramatist, and aggressive controversialist, was educated by the Carmelites in Norwich, and at Jesus College, Cambridge. Until 1533 he was a Carmelite friar, but in that year (a notable one for marriages), he 'was ready for an open breach with Rome. He ascribes his conversion to the influence of Lord Wentworth, but makes no secret of the fact that it coincided with his desire to marry' (McKisack 12). He came to the attention of Cromwell, who protected him from the consequences of his outspokenness from pulpit and stage; upon Cromwell's fall in 1540 he fled to Europe, where, from various Protestant centres, he continued his controversial writings. It was during this period that he arranged for the printing of Grimald's plays. On Edward's accession he returned to England, staying for a while with John Foxe at the Duchess of Richmond's. In 1552 he was offered the 'conveniently distant' bishopric of Ossory in Ireland (McKisack 13), where he rapidly made himself extremely unpopular through his reforming zeal. On Mary's accession he once more went into exile in Europe, returning in 1559. He was nominated to a prebendary in Canterbury, which he took up in February 1560. Here, under the wing of that other noted bibliophile and antiquarian Archbishop Parker, he threw himself into the tasks of gathering materials for an English history, and trying to recover his book collection. He also rapidly embroiled himself in quarrels with local citizens, incidents illustrating his 'irascible vigor in his old age' and 'his urgent need to preach' (Fairfield 147). Although widely known as 'Bilious Bale,' the combative reformer evidently commanded personal affection as well as respect for his zeal, energy, and learning. The tone of Googe's poem is warm, and curiously indulgent.

In 1563 this poem is printed in alternate lines of 4 and 6 syllables.

9–10 *Don Plato's part*: This tradition of Plato's manner of death is disseminated through Cicero's *De senectute* v 13. Thomas Newton (best known for collecting the translations of Seneca's plays) translated this treatise in 1568–9, publishing it first in 1569 under the title *The worthy book of old age*. It had also been translated by Caxton in 1481 and by Robert Whittington in ?1535, but Newton disparages earlier efforts.

19 To M. Edward Cobham.

Brother of Henry Cobham (see below), he was the tenth son of George Brooke, sixth Lord Cobham. Panofsky comments on this poem: 'The underlying convention of the friend as moral guide has created a means of personalizing a theme-poem or precept-poem. These poems are often pleasing in the glimpse they give of personal and social exchanges; presumably this heightened the value of the collection for the contemporary reader as well. Surely many or most of these poems were actually presented at some appropriate occasion.' He cites as parallels Chaucer's envoys to Scogan and Bukton (139).

In 1563 this poem is printed in alternate lines of 4 and 6 syllables, except for lines 33 and 35, which are broken 5 and 5, and the last line of twelve syllables, split 4 and 8.

1–16 *Old Socrates ... doth fail*: the most familiar source in the mid sixteenth century for this anecdote about the famous philosopher is the *Apophthegmata* of Erasmus: 'He exhorted young springals, ever now and then earnestly to view and behold themselves in a glass: to the end, that if they were beautiful and of good feature of body they should beware to commit nothing uncomely for the same: if otherwise, that the defaults of the body might with exercise or furniture of the wit, and with honesty of manners and behaviour be redubbed. So duly did that gay man (of all manner things) promptly take occasion to advise and exhort all persons to the earnest applying of virtue' (*Apophthegms* I 47, trans Udall ciiiv).

20 *towardness*: natural aptitude and good disposition

22 *pretend*: portend, presage

23 *appears*: The editorial emendation from 'appeare' is made for the sake of the rhyme, and on the analogy of the press-variant correction of 'breedes' to *breede* in 21a.4 (F2V).

26 *smally*: not much, very little
32 *prest*: ready, at hand
41 *noughty*: bad, worthless

20 Of Edwards of the Chapel.
Richard Edwards (?1523–1566), playwright, musician, and poet, was a gentleman of the Chapel Royal from 1553, and from 27 October 1561 Master of the Children of the Chapel Royal. He had been a scholar and fellow of Corpus Christi College, Oxford (BA 1544) and student of Christ Church, Oxford (MA 1547), where, as F.P. Wilson notes, 'he must have come in touch with Grimald and his *Archipropheta*' (111 n4). His only extant play, *Damon and Pithias*, was acted before the Queen at Whitehall probably during the Christmas season of 1564–5, and a lost play of *Palamon and Arcite* was acted before the Queen at Oxford in 1566 shortly before his death. Nothing is known of the dramatic productions that must have excited Googe's admiration. Edwards achieved posthumous fame as a poet upon the publication of his anthology of verses by himself and others as *The Paradise of Dainty Devices* (1576), which judging by the number of editions was the most popular Elizabethan poetical miscellany. Googe's work, unless hidden among anonymous or unidentified poems, is not represented. There are two epitaphs on the death of Edwards in Turbervile's *Epitaphs* (1567), one by Thomas Twine, and one by Turbervile (L4v–L6 and T5v–T6). Turbervile's poem echoes both Googe's poem on Edwards, and his epitaph for Grimald.

In 1563 this poem is printed in alternate lines of 4 and 6 syllables.

1 *Camenes*: 'The .ix. Muses' (Cooper). Sir James Frazer, in a note to the Loeb edition of Ovid's *Fasti* III 275, identifies the Camenae as 'water-nymphs whose spring flowed in a sacred grove outside the Porta Capena; but these came to be identified with the Muses.' Grimald uses the same nomenclature in 'The Death of Zoroas' (Tottel no 165).

4 *feres*: equals, peers

9 *Plautus*: (c254–c184 BC). 'A comical poet, born in Umbria: when he had spent all his substance on player's garments, and thereby was brought to extreme poverty, he was fain for his living to serve a baker in turning a quern, or handmill. When he was vacant from that labour, he wrote most eloquent and pleasant comedies, wherein he was reputed so excellent, that Epius Stolo said of him, he doubted not, but that the Muses would speak as Plautus did write, if they should speak Latin. He was in the time of Cato Censorius' (Cooper).

11 *Terence*: (c190–?159 BC.) 'The most eloquent writer of comedies' (Cooper).

21 To L. Blundeston.
In 1563 this poem is printed in alternate lines of 4 and 6 syllables.
3 *cheese from chalk*: proverbial: *ODEP* 113; Tilley C218. Compare Palingenius: 'Why is not Chalk for Cheese as well delighting unto thee, / As lying name of Nobleness?' (90)
6 *affections*: feelings as opposed to reason; passions. *OED* aptly cites the Palmer's comment on one of the intemperate characters in Book II of Spenser's *Faerie Queene*: 'Most wretched man, That to affections does the bridle lend.' The Palmer expands on the theme for two stanzas (*FQ* II iv 34–5).

***21a** The Answer of L. Blundeston to the same.
In 1563 this poem is printed in alternate lines of 4 and 6 syllables. A press-variant correction of the break in line 5 is an important indicator of the lineation of the manuscript and of the compositor's lack of familiarity in breaking 10-syllable lines (from *and / happy* to *and hap- / py*).
1–4 *Affections seeks*: For the grammar, see note to 3.3.
2 *Affections ... reprove*: Unbridled passions reject the principle of moderation.

22 To Alexander Neville.
In 1563 this poem is printed in alternate lines of 4 and 6 syllables. A press-variant correction in line 15 (from *him to sing* to *him sing*) regularizes the syllable count.
12 *Takes all for gold*: A play on the proverb: *ODEP* 316; Tilley A146.
17–18 Panofsky compares the familiar, teasing tone of these lines with Chaucer's *Lenvoy de Chaucer a Scogan* (140).

***22a** Alexander Neville's Answer to the same.
11 *powdered sobs*: sobs 'seasoned' with tears. *OED* takes this as a figurative use of the sense 'sprinkled or seasoned with salt or spice.' Neville likes the transposed adjective: compare *gazing eyes*, (25) and *the plungèd mind* (24a.1).
21 *gripe*: the 'clutch' or 'pinch' of something painful
32 *fry*: This line is cited by *OED* as the first example of the application of 'fry' to a strongly burning passion. See also Rubel 236 and note 167.

43–4 *Phoenix ... rare*: proverbial: ODEP 664; Tilley P256

23 To M. Henry Cobham of the most blessed state of Life. Described by the *DNB* as fifth son of George Brooke, sixth Lord Cobham, Henry's dates are there given as ?1538–1604. However, according to Francis Thynne's genealogy of the Cobhams, the sixth Lord Cobham's fifth and sixth sons Henry the elder and Edward the elder both died without issue, and the seventh son Henry the younger is described as 'now living a pensioner, a knight, and one that hath been ambassador ledger in France for her majesty.' Edward the younger is listed as the tenth son (Holinshed 4:796). Henry was knighted at Kenilworth in 1575, and was ambassador resident at Paris from 1579–83 (*DNB* 4:610–11). The Cobhams were among the most important noble families resident in Kent (Clark 6–7), and it is likely that the brothers were a part of Googe's circle of friends while he was living with his grandmother. Henry was also in Spain at the time of Googe's visit of 1561–2; he was a member of the embassy of Sir Thomas Chaloner, and carried despatches for him (*DNB*). (For Googe's connection with Chaloner in Madrid, see Introduction, pp 13–14). The poem is on a very familiar theme, with many analogues. Compare Surrey's 'The meanes to attain happy life' and Wyatt's 'Of the meane and sure estate,' translating Martial and Seneca respectively (Tottel nos 27, 118), and also Tottel nos 170, 191, 200, all of the mean or poor estate. Googe's poem could be seen as a distillation of Wyatt's three famous satires 'Of the meane and sure estate,' 'Of the Courtiers life,' and 'How to use the Court' (Tottel nos 124–6). Hankins compares this poem with Turbervile's 'To his Friend Francis Th[ynne] leading his life in the country at his desire' (491). The poem is cited by Panofsky as an example of the figure *hirmus*: 'a lengthy structure of suspended grammar and meaning which Puttenham calls '*Irmus*' ... or 'the Long loose' ... The device presents a copious heaping of details. It is used by Googe to suggest a full survey of a subject' (77).

The metrical pattern of this poem is octosyllabic alternately rhymed quatrains. In 1563 the lines are printed broken, usually in 4 and 4 syllables, but with many variations: lines 4, 11, 21–4, and 29 are broken 3 and 5; lines 17, 31, and 33 are broken 5 and 3; and line 26 is broken 2 and 6. Since there is a substantive press-variant at 13 (*I well do mind* instead of *Remembrest thou*?) it is perhaps surprising that no line corrections were made, in view of the correction to 21a.5.

10 *gawn*: This line has a special entry in OED under "† Gawne":

'App[arently] a late spelling of *gone* GANE v.' 'Gane' means 'to open the mouth wide, to gape or yawn.'

11 *Caiser*: Kaiser, emperor. The older spelling emphasizes the connection with Latin Caesar. Googe may be partly playing on the common alliterative phrase 'king or kaiser.'

13–16 Perhaps Wyatt: see Tottel nos 119 and 125.

20 *sturdy*: fierce, violent

21 *Bacchus*: 'The son of Jupiter and Semele, who first invented making of wines, and counted therefore for the God of wine' (Googe 'A Table'). The festival of Bacchus, the Bacchanalia, has become synonymous with drunken revelry.

22 *Venus hath defect*: Lustfulness is wanting (absent). Stephens finds the usage odd, and comments: 'Googe may be playing on the meaning "eclipse" or "failure to shine"' (35). See also note to 12.107–8.

23–4 *Thraso ... Gnatho*: The boastful soldier and the flatterer or parasite in Terence's comedy *Eunuchus*.

24 To Alexander Neville of the blessed State of him that feels not the force of Cupid's flames.

In 1563 this poem is printed in alternate lines of 4 and 6 syllables, except for line 3, which is broken 5 and 5.

3 *Furies*: See note to 1.57.

3 *blinded elf*: Cupid: see note to 10.70.

24a Alexander Neville's Answer to the same.

1 *The plungèd mind*: Compare 22a.11, and note.

25 To Mistress A.

This poem recalls Wyatt's 'The Lover complayneth the unkindness of his love' ('My lute awake'; Tottel no 87). Both poems emphasize the conventional topic of the lady's cruelty, and the threat of age. Googe lacks the lute, but adds the fierce wild animal images, and the Gorgon simile. Compare also Wyatt's 'The lover forsaketh his unkinde love' (Tottel no 100). Turbervile's 'Of the divers and contrary passions and affections of his love' 29–76, according to Hankins, is 'a general paraphrase' of Googe's poem (500).

15 'Like mother, like child': ODEP 546; Tilley M1199.

25 *Gorgon*: 'Gorgons were three sisters, vile and horrible furies in hell with hairs of crawling snakes whereof the one called Medusa was slain by Perseus, Jupiter's bastard' (Googe 'A Table'). The most

beautiful Medusa was punished with snake-locks by Minerva, presumably for having attracted Neptune's sacrilegious rape (Ovid *Metamorphoses* IV 794–803).

46 *time and end*: Although this looks like a misprint for 'time an end,' it is probably a deliberate conflation of two proverbs: 'The end tries all' (*ODEP* 221; Tilley E116) and 'Time tries truth' (*ODEP* 825; Tilley T338) or 'Time tries all things' (*ODEP* 825; Tilley T336).

49–56 Compare Ovid *Ars amatoria* III 69–74.

26 To George Holmedon of a running Head.

TITLE *running*: volatile, flighty, giddy. Googe's use antedates *OED*'s first recorded example of 1571. Panofsky cites this poem as an example of the abuse of the figure *hirmus* (see note to 23), stating 'Most phrases here are merely redundant' (78). It seems likely that this redundancy is intentionally used by Googe to make the point of his jest. Hudson several times pointed out that he regarded this poem and 'Unhappy tongue' (34) as 'true sonnets in the modern sense' (293–4); but see Introduction p 23.

In 1563 this poem is printed in alternate lines of 4 and 6 syllables, with the exception of lines 3 and 10, which are broken 5 and 5.

14 *Physician*: A variant on 'Physician, heal thyself' (Luke 4.23, and proverbial: see *ODEP* 622; Tilley P267).

27 To the Translation of Palingen.

One of Googe's poems most often singled out for praise. Clay Hunt calls it 'one of the best examples in the early Elizabethan period of the intimate, conversational style of familiar verse' (278).

11 *Muses*: See note to 16.17.

11 *feres*: companions

28 Heart Absent.

In 1563 this poem is printed in alternate lines of 4 and 6 syllables, except for line 16, which is broken 5 and 5.

13 *daw*: jackdaw, used figuratively for a simpleton

15–16 *And where ... Aesop's ass*: These lines are obscure. What is the referent for *they*? His heart, senses, and wisdom? The fable referred to appears to be that of the Ass who enviously tries to behave like a cossetted pet dog, and approaching his master to 'make cheer' to him, 'leapt upon his shoulders and began to kiss and lick him. The lord then began to cry out with a high voice and said. Let this foul whoreson which hurteth me so sore be beaten and put away'

(Aesop lxiii). The sense appears to be that the lover's attempts to ingratiate himself are merely annoying to his beloved and harmful to himself. See Sheidley (1981) 132 n55.

29 To Alexander Neville.
Ovid Remedia amoris 139–40, 161–2. The first couplet is translated by Sir Thomas Elyot in *The Governor* I xxvi of exercises other than hunting and dancing that are not 'repugnant to virtue'; 'it were much better to be occupied in honest recreation than to do nothing' (88). The second couplet is cited in Mirandula's *Illustrium poetarum flores* under 'De desidia.' See also Googe's sixth eclogue, 93–6.
5 *Aegisthus*: Left in charge of the kingdom of Argos when Agamemnon went to the Trojan war, Aegisthus fell in love and lived with Agamemnon's wife. Their murder of Agamemnon upon his return set in train yet another sequence of disasters of this calamitous family.

***29a** The Answer of A. Neville to the same.
The terms of Neville's answer recall both the psychological allegory of Blundeston's prefatory poem and Googe's moral allegory of the sin-drowned soul in his eighth eclogue.

30 To Mistress D.
Perhaps his future wife, Mary Darrell.
1 *Cytherian*: of the island of Cythera; an epithet of Venus, the *lady* of the next line, because she was supposed to have risen from the waves off Cythera. In referring to a high hill, Googe may be thinking of Cithaeron, a hill in Thessaly variously supposed sacred to Bacchus, or to Jupiter and the Muses. His intention may be to unite ideas of love and poetry, and also to play on the opposition of hill and Dungeon, which is in fact topographically paradoxical (see the following note). In the early sixteenth-century poem *The Court of Love*, first published in the 1561 edition of Chaucer's *Works*, the Court of Love is located 'A lite beside the mount of Citharee' (Skeat 410).
6 *the Dungeon*: Googe is punning on the name of his grandmother's house, the manor called the Dungeon after the large artificial hill adjoining the old walls of Canterbury. The manor (pulled down in 1752) was situated close to the accompanying lesser mount. The spelling of the name varied, a popular interpretation being 'Danejohn,' a fortification built either by or against the Danes (Hasted 11:121–2, 147–51).

7 *Pluto*: 'The god of hell, otherwise called the devil' (Googe 'A Table')
8 *Proserpine*: 'Wife to Pluto and lady of hell' (Googe 'A Table')

31 Out of an old Poet.
The old Poet has not been identified. The substance of the poem suggests that the speaker might be Seneca's Phaedra (in *Hippolytus*), or Ovid's Myrrha (*Metamorphoses* X 311–514), both of whom debate with themselves their incestuous lust, but there is no clear verbal correspondence.

In 1563 this poem is printed in alternate lines of 4 and 6 syllables.

32 [untitled]
This and the next two poems, all lacking titles, may be intended to fall under the heading 'Out of an old Poet.' The story of the fly and the candle has an unexpected twist, since usually the 'butterfly' (nowadays a moth) is presented as an emblem of man's self-destructive pursuit of pleasure. See, for example, the English translation of Paradin, entitled *Heroicall Devises* Y2V–3. See also *ODEP* 271; Tilley F394. In the Trinity College, Cambridge copy of the 1563 edition, marginal additions and alterations in a late seventeenth- or eighteenth-century hand convert the first twelve lines of Googe's poulter's measure into octosyllabic lines. The result is as follows:

Once musing as I sat, alone
with fire and candle burning by,
When all were hushed I might discern
a poor and simple seely fly,
That flew about before mine eyes
with merry free rejoicing heart,
And here and there with wings did play
as one both void of pain and smart.
Sometimes by me she down would sit
when once that she had played her fill
And ever when she rested had
about the ⟨flame⟩ room she flittered still.

4 *seely*: innocent, harmless

33 [untitled]
The power of the *caro nome* has been celebrated at least from Petrarch

(for example, sonnet 5) to *Rigoletto*. Compare Sidney *Astrophil and Stella* sonnets 52 and 55.

34 [untitled]

Peirce comments: 'the poem is obviously an imitation of a sonnet (No. 48 of the *Miscellany*) that Wyatt translated from Petrarch's sonetto in vita 34' (355). On the 'sonnet' form of this poem, see note to 26 above. Hankins states that Turbervile's 'The Lover blames his Tongue that failed to utter his suit in time of need' is modelled on Googe's poem, and cites also Thomas Howell's 'He accuseth his tongue' (502).

In 1563 this poem is printed in alternate lines of 4 and 6 syllables, except for lines 7 and 13, where Googe's habit of elision has caused two mistakes in breaking the line: in 7, the break occurs after *and*, and in 13 after *is*. In each case failure to note the elision (pity^and, she^is) gives 7 syllables in the second half line.

10 *plaints*: For the editorial emendation, see note to 19.23.

35 Oculi augent dolorem.
Out of sight, out of mind.

Oculi aguent dolorem: 'Eyes intensify grief' or 'seeing increases sorrow' (Cicero *Ep. ad fam.* VI 1 ad Torq 1). This popular snippet from Cicero could be found in such handy collections as P. Lagnerius's frequently reprinted *M. Tull. Ciceronis sententiae illustriores, Apophthegmata* ... in the Lyon, 1547 edition, this phrase is Item 181 of the Sententiae.

Out of sight, out of mind: proverbial: ODEP 602; Tilley S348

This poem is an example of 'Clymax. or the Marching figure,' explained and illustrated by Puttenham in his *Arte of English Poesie* (207–8). 'Upon consideracion of the state of this lyfe he wisheth death' (Tottel no 174), uses the figure to expound on a graver subject. Rollins cites as parallels Googe and Turbervile. Turbervile's poem is an answer to Googe's:

To Master Googe his Sonnet out of sight out of thought.

The less I see, the more my teen [suffering],
The more my teen, the greater grief,
The greater grief, the lesser seen,
The lesser seen, the less relief,
The less relief, the heavier sprite,
When P. is farthest out of sight.

The rarer seen, the rifer sobs,
The rifer sobs, the sadder heart,
The sadder heart, the greater throbs,
The greater throbs, the worser smart,
The worser smart proceeds of this:
That I my P. so often miss.
The nearer to, the more I smile,
The more I smile, the merrier mind,
The merrier mind doth thought exile,
And thought exiled, recourse I find
Of heavenly joys: all this delight
Have I when P. is once in sight.

(*Epitaphes* R3r–v)

18 *depart*: part, separate

36 [untitled]

This poem is printed in Turbervile's *Epitaphs* and is followed by 'Turbervile's answer':

Not God (friend Googe) the Lover blames
as worker of his woes:
But Cupid that his fiery flames
so franticly bestows (C2).

37 [untitled]

This poem is printed in Turbervile's *Epitaphes* and is followed by 'Turbervile's answer and distich to the same':

Two lines shall teach you how
to purchase ease anew:
Let reason rule where Love did reign
and idle thoughts eschew (B7v).

Panofsky cites this poem as an example of the 'sententious truisms' of mid-Tudor amatory poetry: 'Googe's couplet is a love-sentence, an entry in a possible phrase-book. He does not distinguish between public and private; he assumes that significant experience is common to all men. Googe's assumption of a moral context which describes the life of passion as unsettling, contradictory, and ultimately defeating directly determines his poetic surface, its generalized language and sententious form' (157).

38 Of the unfortunate choice of his Valentine.
Turbervile also has a poem 'of the choice of his Valentine': like Googe, he fails to draw his lady's scroll. However, the name is the same (though the lady is not equally beautiful), and this coincidence happily recalls to his memory the image of his absent love (*Epitaphes* Q6). On the drawing of names as a Valentine's Day custom, see Chambers 1:255–7; on Valentine's Day observances in a literary context, see Stevens 184–6.
1 *Furies*: See note to 1.57.
2 *Limbo lake*: the pit of hell; according to OED this usage, and that of 'lake' for pit, or den of lions, derives from Latin *lacus*. The first example of Limbo-lake given in OED is from Phaer's translation of Virgil's *Aeneid*. The associations for Googe are probably more classical than medieval religious.
19 *draught*: act of drawing (the paper)
20 *pallèd*: Modern senses of appalled, dismayed, suit the context better than OED enfeebled, weakened.

39 The uncertainty of Life.
3–10 Biblical, Christian, and classical authors unite in warning against the brevity, fragility, and vanity of life. (Langius's *Polyanthea* [1613] provides an impressive summary of examples under VITA). A couple of favourite classical sayings are: 'nil homini certum est' (Naught is certain for man: Ovid *Tristia* v v 27); 'vitae summa brevis spem nos vetat incohare longam' (life's brief span forbids thy entering on far-reaching hopes: Horace *Odes* I iv 15).
11–12 *As tail of eel*: See Whiting E48: 'As if thou woldest an eel or laumprun holde with streite handis, how myche strengerli thou thristis, so myche the sunnere it shal sliden away' (*WBible Job Prologue* I 671 [1–3]); and E45: 'Worldly trust is as slipir as an eel' (*Lerne to Die* 205.726). Compare also Surrey's 'The frailtie and hurtfulnes of beautie' (Tottel no 9): 'Slipper in sliding as is an eles taile / Harde to attaine, once gotten not geason.'
14 *it*: presumably death, not yet mentioned

41 Of Mistress D.S.
In 1563 this poem is printed in alternate lines of 4 and 6 syllables.
1 *filèd*: polished
2 *Diane*: goddess of chastity
7 *Good S.*: evidently a disyllabic name

42 Of Money.

Googe's variation on an extremely familiar theme has a charming lightness. (For a survey of the theme see Mills *One Soul in Bodies Twain*; the title is taken from Grimald's poem 'Of Friendship,' Tottel no 154.) Richard Taverner's version of Erasmus's commentary on the proverb 'Ubi amici, ibi opes' gives much the same message in a more embittered tone:

Where friends be, there be goods. By this is meant that friends be better than money, and that unto the sustentation of man's life, friends be more available without money, than money without friends. And for this cause among the Scythians (as Lucian declareth) he was counted the richest man, which had the surest and best friends. But now if a man will have respect to the manners of these days, we had need to turn the proberb and say, where goods be, there be friends (*Proverbes* B5v–6).

Turbervile presents the conventional point of view in his answer poem to Googe:

To Master Googe's fancy that begins Give money me, take friendship whoso list.

Friend Googe, give me the faithful friend to trust,
And take the fickle coin fro [1567 for] me that lust.
For friends in time of trouble and distress
With help and sound advice will soon redress
Each growing grief that gripes the pensive breast,
When money lies locked up in covert chest.
Thy coin will cause a thousand cares to grow,
Which if thou hadst no coin thou couldst not know.
Thy friend no care but comfort will procure;
Of him thou mayst at need thyself assure.
Thy money makes the thief in wait to lie,
Whose fraud thy friend and falsehood will descry.
Thou canst not keep unlocked thy careful coin
But some from thee thy money will purloin:
Thy faithful friend will never start aside,
But take his share of all that shall betide,
When thou art dead thy money is bereft,
But after life thy trusty friend is left:
Thy money serves another master then,

Thy faithful friend links with none other man.
So that, friend Googe, I deem it better, I,
To choose the friend and let the money lie.

(*Epitaphes* Q2r–v)

In 1563 Googe's poem is printed in alternate lines of 4 and 6 syllables, except for lines 1 and 4, which are broken 5 and 5.
8 *louring*: dark and threatening, gloomy

43 Going towards Spain.
With this poem and 'Coming homeward out of Spain,' compare Wyatt's 'Of his returne from Spaine' (Tottel no 121).
2–4 *Brutus*: The mythological Trojan founder of Britain. See, for example, Holinshed and the earlier chroniclers Grafton and Stow, or Spenser's *FQ* II x 9–13. For a brief summary of the development of the story, see Rollins and Baker 3. Cooper, in the entry on 'Britannia,' argues strongly against the legend, but Googe is clearly fond of it.
5 *lusty*: possibly 'fertile,' although OED gives only one example, in 1601. Stephens glosses 'massive'; OED gives an example of 1641 for the first use of this sense.
9 *cark*: to labour anxiously, to toil and moil
11–12 *take all … the net*: Compare 'All is fish that comes to the net' *ODEP* 264; Tilley A136.

44 At Bonneval in France.
Compare Surrey's 'The fansie of a wearied lover' (Tottel no 36), and Wyatt's 'The lover that fled love now folowes it with his harme' (Tottel no 71). Peirce also compares Wyatt's 'Of disapointed purpose by negligence' (Tottel no 120) (373). The situation in the poem could be seen as the failure of the advice given by Ovid *Remedia amoris* 213–18. Peirce comments: 'The poem is obviously an exercise in rhetoric as well as an imitation of mood. The two quatrains combine several figures: besides the usual alliteration and epithets, one finds *ecphonesis* in the first and eighth lines, *anaphora* in the repetition of "When," *hirmus* in the series of subordinate clauses, which also incorporate *synonymia* as they rephrase the nature of the illness, and *erotema* in the unanswered, rhetorical question' (374).

In 1563 the poem is printed in alternate lines of 4 and 6 syllables, except for the first line, which is broken 5 and 5.
TITLE Bonneval is a town south-west of Paris, near Chartres, on the central overland route from England to Spain.

9 *Charybdis*: 'A dangerous gulf between Calabria and Sicily' (Googe 'A Table')
10 *Scylla*: 'The daughter of Nisus, king of the Megarenses. It is also a great and dangerous rock in the sea by Sicily' (Googe 'A Table'). The Scylla who became a rock is the daughter of Typhon, but both Virgil (*Eclogues* VI 74–7) and Ovid (*Fasti* IV 500) conflate the two. Scylla and Charybdis as inescapable alternative dangers early became proverbial: see ODEP 707; Tilley S169.

45 Coming homeward out of Spain.
Compare Wyatt's 'Of his returne from Spaine' (Tottel no 121).
In 1563 this poem is printed in alternate lines of 4 and 6 syllables.

46 To L. Blundeston of Ingratitude.
In 1563 this poem is printed in alternate lines of 4 and 6 syllables, with the exception of lines 3 and 10, which are broken 5 and 5.
1–2 *the tender marlion ... lark to prey*: References to the story of the marlion or merlin, a species of falcon, and the lark are plentiful. See, for example, Tottel no 173, 'The Lover sheweth his wofull state, and prayeth pitye.' Rollins cites four parallels, beginning with Googe (in Tottel 2:260–1). The story is used in a moralized poem of c1325 on God's mercy, entitled by Carleton Brown, following its refrain, 'Mercy passes all things' (125–31). It is found in the compendium of anecdotes for sermons by Robert Holcot known as *Convertimini* (see Herbert 125–6). Most of the manuscripts listed by Herbert assign the story to 'Plinius de mirabilibus mundi'; two (Harley 5369 and 5396) seem uncertain, referring instead to a mysterious 'pollunius' or 'polunque' (presumably misreadings of 'Plinius'). I have not been able to find the story in Pliny. Chaucer refers to the story twice, in *The Parliament of Fowls* 339–40, and in *Troilus and Criseyde* III 1191–2. See also lines 585–90 of the seventh day of the first week of Du Bartas's *Divine Weeks and Works* (1:310).
21 *eager*: fierce, savage
21 *hungered*: famished, starved
29 *Lo ... here, how*: This passage provides an acute example of the problems of modernizing spelling and punctuation. The original, 'Loe, *Blundeston* heare / how kyndenes doth habounde,' would allow the reading 'hear how'; the choice made takes *Lo, here* as 'see in this instance,' rather than interpreting 'Now, hear this statement.'

***46a** The Answer of L. Blundeston to the same.

In 1563 this poem is printed in alternate lines of 4 and 6 syllables, except for the hypermetrical line 5. Without this parenthesis, the form of the poem coincides with that of the English sonnet.

1 *This mirror*: a mirror in the sense of that which 'exhibits something to be imitated' rather than 'reflects something to be avoided'

6–13 I have not been able to find any parallels for the story of the pike's ingratitude to the tench, but the pike's unnatural cruelty as shown in devouring its own young was frequently mentioned from Aristotle on, and found its way into Renaissance emblem books (Henkel and Schöne 698; I am indebted to Professor Beryl Rowland for suggesting that the emblem books might provide illumination of this oddity of natural history).

12 *chirurgeon*: a surgeon

15 *pound*: a body of still water, usually of artificial formation, a pond. Also an enclosure for fish, but the first example of this sense in OED is in 1809.

47 To the Tune of Appelles.

The Tune of Appelles has not been identified (it does not appear in Simpson's *The British Broadside Ballad and its Music*), but it is frequently mentioned, especially between 1560 and 1580, as Bruce Pattison notes (167). It apparently took its name from an unidentified popular song, and continued to be used for ballads and 'courtly' lyrics, in the manner discussed by Stevens (54, 77, 127–8). In 1565–6 a ballad is registered to Wm Griffith called 'Appelles and Pygmalyne to the tune of ye fyrst Appelles' and another to Alex Lacy 'Appelles with an other Dytty' (Rollins *Index* nos 90, 91); the latter may be found in Huth's *Ancient Ballads and Broadsides*. Other ballads and poems to be sung 'To the tune of Appelles' include the ballad 'The Plagues of Northumberland,' printed by Thomas Colwell (see Huth, and Lilly; Thomas Howell's 'lamentable historie of Sephalus with the Unfortunat end of Procris' (in *Newe Sonets and Pretie Pamphlets* licensed to Thomas Colwell 1567–8; in *Poems* 146); and 'The lover being wounded with his Ladis beutie, requireth mercy' in *A Handful of Pleasant Delights* (1584) 55). What these narrative, political, or amatory poems have in common is, of course, their stanza form: six octosyllabic lines, rhyming ababcc. Googe's poem is drawn from Montemayor's 'To heare me wearied is the cleerest river' (*Diana* 54–5; Lopez Estrada 66–8), and provides an interesting example of his freedom with his sources. At times he translates fairly closely, but in general he is recasting and even rearranging Montemayor's ideas. Googe's first two stanzas are drawn from Montemayor's first; his third, fourth, and fifth are loosely based on ideas drawn from Montemayor's second and third; his sixth and seventh are almost a translation of Montemayor's fourth, except that Googe has substituted 'Nature' for the unspecified creative force questioned by Montemayor, and has introduced the notion of a provident being. Googe's last stanza is different in application from Montemayor's, being a confident plea for mercy rather than a despairing complaint against cruelty, but his phrasing is reminiscent of Montemayor's. Peirce comments that this poem is 'different from anything else in the volume' and that 'it is the kind of song that one finds shepherd lovers singing throughout the sixteenth-century romances. An unusually lyrical poem for Googe, it makes a very pleasant conclusion to all the "sonnets," and particularly to the fifteen short poems dealing with love' (361–2, 363).

35 *alablaster*: alabaster; *OED* comments that this usual sixteenth–seventeenth-century spelling was apparently due to a confusion with 'arblaster,' a cross-bowman, also written 'alablaster.'

37 *devise*: imagine, guess

48 Cupido Conquered.

This poem combines the venerable traditions of the dream vision and the psychomachia. The poet/narrator seeks to ease his amorous woe by the pleasant sights and sounds of springtime. Because of his service of the Muses, he is taken by Mercury to the castle of Diana, and becomes a spectator of the overthrow of the forces of Cupid by Diana's army under her captain Hippolytus. Googe was evidently familiar with the works collected under the name of his admired Chaucer, but his departure from his models is evident in his title: dream vision poems are usually concerned with the attainment or at least the service of love, not with its conquest. For a lengthy analysis of the poem, see Sheidley (1972) 150–66.

1–68 The May setting, with its flowers and birds and joyous renewal contrasting with the sad state of the lover, is a popular convention of the poetry of dream vision and love complaint at least from the time of *The Romance of the Rose*. Googe knew the Chaucerian translation of parts of this vastly influential poem well enough to quote an extensive passage in *The Ship of Safeguard*. A poem which uses the same tradition, Surrey's 'Complaint of a lover, that defied love, and was by love after the more tormented' (Tottel no 5), provides a close parallel to Googe's description of the state of the lover, of his response to the joys of spring, of the birdsong and the lover's sententious disquisition on it.

40 *Amphion*: 'The son of Jupiter, and king of Thebes, whom the Poets feigned first to invent music, and thereby to raise the walls of Thebes' (Googe 'A Table')

43 *Sir Orpheus*: 'A Thracian, son of Apollo, so far excelling in Music, that he moved stones, trees, and blocks with his pleasant harmony. By Music also he brought his wife out of hell, and was after torn in pieces by women, some think destroyed with lightning' (Googe 'A Table').

45 *Apollo*: 'He is counted God of Music, physic, poetry, and shooting: and hath by poets given him a triple name and power. In heaven he is called Sol, in earth Liber pater, in hell Apollo' (Cooper).

48 *borne … bell*: proverbial: see ODEP 44; Tilley B275.

49 *the Thracian*: Orpheus

70 *a stately laurel tree*: Googe's laurel tree and fountain are more natural than the golden and bejewelled laurels and fountain where Orpheus sat in Diana's temple (*Diana* p 143, l 18–p 144 l 2). In Palingenius's Virgo, when the poet is instructed by 'Jove his daughter dear,' 'Beside a spring we both sat down, and under laurel shade' (87).

79–122 For the trees and birds, see, for example, the translation of the *Romance of the Rose* attributed to Chaucer 105–8, 492–508.

94 *raught*: reached

107 *Sir Phoebus*: See note to 5.1.

112 *Byblis*: 'The daughter of Miletus, who being enamoured on her own brother Caunus, and of him neglected, died for sorrow' (Cooper). She was turned into a fountain (Ovid *Metamorphoses* IX 454–665).

114 *Narcissus*: The story of the beautiful youth who pined away from frustrated love for his own image reflected in a spring, eventually turning into the flower that bears his name, is memorably told by Ovid (*Metamorphoses* III 402–510). Among poets in the sixteenth century fascinated by its powerful psychological and philosophical resonances was Spenser, who used the key phrase '*inopem me copia fecit*' (466; 'The very abundance of my riches beggars me,' or 'plenty makes me poore') as the 'Embleme' of his September eclogue, as well as in *Amoretti* XXXV and *The Faerie Queene* I iv 29. See also the Chaucerian version of the *Romance of the Rose* 1462–1538.

125 *the woody nymphs*: the Dryads. The first example of 'woody' in

the sense of belonging to the woods given in OED is 1590 Spenser FQ I vi 18 'The wooddy Nymphes, faire Hamadryades.'

131–49 *A person ... Mercury ... son of Maia*: 'The son of Jupiter by Maia, whom poets feign to have wings on his head and feet, to signify that talk (which is represented by the person of Mercury) doth quickly pass through the air. He is feigned to be messenger of the Gods, because by speech and words all things are declared. He was compted God of eloquence, merchandise, feats of activity, and theft also' (Cooper). Virgil attributes his power to his rod (*virga*, the Caduceus: *Aeneid* IV 242–6), but it is usually described as twined with snakes, rather than made of gold. For the story of how Mercury stole Io by lulling Argus to sleep with his reed-pipe, his eloquence and his 'charmed rod, with which he bringeth things a sleepe,' see Ovid *Metamorphoses* I 668–721 (in Golding's translation 671–2).

153 *Muses all of Helicon*: See note to 16.17.

162 *Momus*: See note to 1.39.

173–80 *him that thundered out*: Thomas Phaer; see 15 and headnote.

174 *Anchises' son*: Aeneas

175 *Maro*: Virgil

181–4 *Mark him ... agone*: William Baldwin, compiler of *The Mirror for Magistrates* (see the edition of Lily B. Campbell, especially 21–4). Baldwin is named with Googe and others by Heywood among the 'finest wits' of the Inns of Court in the Preface to Seneca's *Thyestes* (London 1560) *7v–8.

185–8 *Mark him ... penned*: probably Alexander Neville, noted here for his translation of Seneca's *Oedipus*, but perhaps John Studley: see the praise of Googe, Neville, and others in 'T.B. to the Reader' in Studley's translation of Seneca's *Agamemnon* (London 1566).

199 *Diana*: 'The daughter of Jupiter, which fleeing the company of men, to the intent that she would not be moved with carnal lusts, did continually exercise herself in hunting wild beasts, and for her chaste life was honoured of the Paynims for a goddess' (Cooper).

205 *the ladies nine*: the Muses

207 *the blinded God*: Cupid: see note to 10.70.

221–36 The flying survey, and the tone of delighted amusement, may owe something to Chaucer's *House of Fame*, though Googe is better off with his own wings than carried in the 'clawes starke' of Chaucer's eagle, who is an even more daunting and impatient aerial companion than Mercury.

224 *flow*: obsolete past tense of 'fly'

249–50 *that fell unhappy fiend ... light*: Mercury

261–4 *Ptolemy … globe … stand*: The famous second-century mathematician, astronomer, and geographer is much used by William Cuningham in his *Cosmographical Glasse* (London 1559), especially in the third book when explaining how to set forth 'the platform of th'universal face of th'earth' by means of a compass card or globe.
281–324 Compare Felicia's palace, the Temple of Diana, in Montemayor's *Diana*, especially p 133 ll 25–9 and p 142 l 16–p 143 l 18.
286 *portured*: painted
287–300 *Orion*: 'The son of Neptune, a famous hunter, who desiring the company of Diana, was slain of a scorpion, and after canonized among the stars' (Googe 'A Table'). More bluntly, Orion 'would have deflowered Diana' (Cooper).
314 *Acteon*: For the story of the fate Acteon met for coming upon Diana as she bathed in a woodland pool, see Ovid *Metamorphoses* III 155–252.
315 *totorn*: past tense of 'to-tear,' to tear to pieces
345–8 *Dido … Hypsipyle … Lucretia … Penelope*: Of these famous women presented by Googe as types of chaste married love, the first three appear in Chaucer's *Legend of Good Women* as martyrs for love. Lucretia and Penelope are instanced by Montemayor among the wonderful engravings on the Obelisk in the temple of Diana (though he mistakenly names Penelope, Medea) (*Diana* p 142 ll 20–1). Penelope, Hypsipyle, and Dido all appear in Ovid's *Heroides*.
345 *Dido*: Dido's passion for Aeneas, which resulted in her suicide when he left her to pursue his Roman destiny, is most familiar from Virgil and Ovid, and *Aeneid* IV and *Heroides* VII in turn form the main sources for Chaucer's 'Legend of Dido.' However, Googe may be referring to the alternate story of Dido, who, when urged to remarry after Sichaeus' death, 'the noble gentlewoman, rather choosing valiantly to die, than to appear to forget the love of her first husband, killed herself.' The passion for Aeneas, that 'Virgil and other poets feign, … by the credit of most certain histories … is convinced to be false' (Cooper).
346 *Hypsipyle*: Queen of Lemnos, she was married to but abandoned by Jason; nevertheless, as Chaucer says, 'trewe to Jason was she al hire lyf, / And ever kepte hire chast, as for his wif' (*Legend of Good Women* 1576–7).
347 *Lucretia*: Shakespeare's poem of the determined Roman woman who killed herself rather than endure the shame of Tarquin's rape is perhaps the best-known treatment of the story today. Googe doubtless knew the versions in Livy and in Ovid's *Fasti*, as well as

in Chaucer, who by additions to his main source (*Fasti* II 725–852), emphasizes Lucretia's heart 'so wyfly and so trewe' that she would not suffer her husband to 'have the foule name' (*Legend of Good Women* 1841–6).

348 *Penelope*: Like Lucretia, Ulysses' wife is very frequently cited for her admirable fidelity and marital chastity.

361–72 *Ismenis ... Psecas*: the nymphs who attended Diana bathing in the fountain when the ill-fated Acteon saw her (Ovid *Metamorphoses* III 169–72). Ismenis is Crocale; Ovid's 'Ismenis Crocale' is usually translated 'Theban Crocale' (or by Golding, 'The Theban Ladie Crocale'; see II 198). Niphe (so named in Golding and Lemprière) appears as Nephele in the Loeb text.

373 *accompanèd*: This form of 'accompanied' is not separately recorded in OED, but it seems possible that Googe was deliberately using an older form. See the citations in OED under 'Accompany' 8, especially c1460: 'Which Ambassatours schal nede to be honorably accompanyd'; and 8b, in particular 1477: 'Covetise hath accompaigned them from their childehode.'

374 *bains*: bathing, baths

379 *Hippolytus*: a familiar type of militant male chastity, renowned in drama and poetry for his devotion to Diana and his resistance to the passion of his stepmother Phaedra. Googe was undoubtedly familiar with Seneca's play *Hippolytus*, with Phaedra's lament in Ovid's *Heroides* IV, and Hippolytus' own description of his martyrdom in Ovid's *Metamorphoses* XV 497–546.

411–30, 585–600 Compare Ovid's *Amores* I ix 1: 'Militat omnis amans, et habet sua castra Cupido' (Every lover is a soldier, and Cupid has a camp of his own).

417 *ride*: possibly a misprint for 'rides'

430 *the wound doth fester still*: Compare Ovid *Remedia amoris* 101–2.

440 *by heap*: in a crowd (OED *sb*. 3, 5)

441–2 *Some ... to rid themselves from strife*: Compare Ovid *Remedia amoris* 17–18.

447–80 For Vulcan's capture and exposure of Mars and Venus in adultery, see Ovid *Metamorphoses* IV 171–89.

495 *fine*: end

565 *Three battles big*: three divisions or battalions of soldiers

585 *Three spies*: The conjectural emendation of *Three* (thre) for 'Thie' is likely because of the similarity of the type for *i* and *r*. The three spies are perhaps the 'three manner of virtues' of the intellectual soul, appropriately assigned to the three battalions of the forces of chastity:

'one is *rationalis*, whereby it taketh heed to the thing that is true: the other is called *concupiscibilis*, whereby it taketh heed to the thing that is good, the third is called *irascibilis*, and thereby it taketh heed to the thing that is great and huge, and to the thing that is everlasting. In the *Rationali* is knowledge of the truth, in *Concupiscibili*, will and desire of good thing: in *Irascibili* is flight of contrary, that is, of evil' (*Batman uppon Bartholome* III 6).

587 *Alongst*: by the side of, close by; the earliest example recorded in OED is 1580.

600–16 Excess combines attributes of gluttony, lechery, and 'greedy Avarice' as well as suggestions of pride and wrath. Compare Spenser's pageant of the Deadly Sins, FQ I iv 18–36, especially 27. Googe's humorously exaggerated portrait also suggests Shakespeare's Ancient Pistol, who in *Henry V* is described as 'swelling like a turkey-cock' (V i 15).

607 *turkey cock*: guinea-fowl, not the American turkey

617 *the blinded god*: Cupid: see note to 10.70.

620 *pesters*: probably 'plagues,' 'infests,' but perhaps with some sense of 'crowds' or 'fills' (see OED *v* †3 and 4a).

621 *triumph*: By Googe's day, the triumphal procession of the victorious commander with the spoils of war had been re-classicized in art by such famous paintings as Mantegna's sequence, but Googe is evoking more the medieval and early Renaissance literary triumphs, most especially Petrarch's very influential *Trionfi* (translated into English in 1554 by Henry Parker, Lord Morley), which were frequently the subjects of paintings.

647 *foggy*: unwholesomely bloated, swollen with flabby and unhealthy corpulence

647 *side*: apparently an adjective meaning 'ample' or possibly 'hanging far down,' although the usage is strange and not recorded in OED: it would seem to be a figurative application of OED 'Side,' *a* in senses 1 or 3.

662 In order to regularize the metre of this line, Thompson conjectures 'that Googe intended the diphthong of *noyse* to represent two syllables' (63 n5).

680 *seely*: helpless, but used scornfully rather than with pity (contrast 5.87).

692 *themself*: 'In Standard English *themself* was the normal form to c1540, but disappeared c1570. *Themselfs*, *themselves* appears c1500, and became the standard form c1540' (*OED*).

699 *Amongst*: of place: together, among something else. Not recorded in OED, but compare 'Among' B *adv* †3.

711–14 *A soldier ... flight*: The metaphor of a charioteer or rider controlling horses for reason governing the wayward animal appetites is frequent and popular since at least Plato's *Phaedrus*. See, for example, Rowland *Blind Beasts* (especially 129–40), and Kolve *Chaucer and the Imagery of Narrative* (especially 239–47). See also the discourse of Arete (Vertue) in Palingenius's Gemini (35).
740 *mate*: OED cites this usage as the first example of the meaning 'A suitable associate (†or adversary); an equal in eminence or dignity.' However, to read *mate* as meaning 'checkmate' makes equally good sense.

SELECTED OTHER WORKS BY GOOGE

Prefatory poem from Nilus Cabasilas.

TITLE *Nilus Cabasilas ... vii hundred years since*: In 1560 the work was not as ancient as the title-page claims. According to the current *Encyclopedia Britannica* 2:702–3, Nilus Cabasilas (c1298–1363) was named metropolitan of Thessalonica in 1361, but died before he could take jurisdiction. His three published works are on the causes of the dissension between Rome and Byzantium, on the fire of purgatory, and this work on the primacy of the Pope. His anti-Rome position made him a favourite of Protestant polemicists, and as late as 1626 his works were drawing refutations from papist supporters (*Enciclopedia Italiana* 8:194).
5 *haughty whore ... Caesar's right*: The whore of Babylon of Revelation 17 was regularly identified by the reformers with the papacy. The Geneva Bible glosses the woman as 'the Antichrist, that is, the Pope with the whole bodie of his filthie creatures,' and the beast she sits on as 'the Romaine empire which being fallen into decay, the whore of Rome usurped autoritie.' The image and its associations are amply explored in Spenser's Duessa (*FQ* I, especially vii 16–18, viii 13–25). Googe later translated Kirchmeyer's *The Popish Kingdome, or reigne of Antichrist* (1570).
13 *Antiquity*: the people (or writers, etc) of ancient times collectively
25 *Finis qp B.G.*: 'The end quoth Barnabe Googe'

The Preface

1–32 *Sir Phebe, Goat, Capricorn, Saturn, Twins, Bull, Boreas*: Googe's references to the sun, to signs of the zodiac, to the planet Saturn,

and to the north wind, identify the time of year as the winter solstice, around 22 December.
35 *Fair Ladies nine*: the muses
46 *Melpomen*: the muse presiding over tragedy, and, for Horace, giving lyric inspiration (*Odes* III xxx, IV iii).
54 *Lucan*: poet of Nero's time, most famous for his poem the *Pharsalia*, of Civil Wars between Caesar and Pompey, a subject viewed here by Googe as a story of a tragic fall.
57 *Urany*: Urania, 'one of the Muses, which is president of Astronomy' (Cooper)
68 *Aratus*: The *Phaenomena* of Aratus is an erstwhile immensely popular Greek astrological poem of the third century BC. Googe probably toyed with the idea of translating one of the many Latin translations or versions, such as the one attributed to Germanicus Caesar.
78–80 *Snake, Bears*: the constellations Draco, Ursa Major, and Ursa Minor
91 *Calliope*: the muse of heroic poetry. For Cooper, she 'excelled all the other in sweetness of voice,' and Googe calls her 'the worthiest sister among the muses' ('A Table').
159 *are*: editorial emendation. The 1560 edition reads 'and.'

The Book to the reader.

6 *yfreight*: laden
19–20 *nose of Rhinocere*: an expression (derived from Latin) used to describe a sneer
27–9 *he … Apelles' shoe*: '*Apelles* a notable man an Ephesian born, who excelled in the Art of painting' (Googe 'A Table'). As Pliny tells the story referred to here, the shoemaker who corrected the famous painter's depiction of a sandal did not betray himself as a carping and foolish critic until he also found fault with the leg (*Natural History* xxxv xxxvi 85).

The Translator to the Reader.

4 *Brutus' line*: See note to 43.2–4.
17–32 *A Poet …Cheril*: Choerilus was a notoriously incompetent Greek epic poet who accompanied Alexander the Great.
36 *coparcener*: co-heir

Dedicatory epistle

30–5 *Hipponax and Bubalus, Tirtaeus, Justin, Alphabet*: Justin refers to the abridged version of the lost history of Trogus Pompeius. The entries in Googe's 'A Table,' which he here calls his *Alphabet*, are as follows:

Bubalus A certain painter who hating one Hipponax a Poet, painted his face his picture lively expressed, to be seen and laughed at of all men. The Poet (not well contented with this malicious deed) with Iambic verses so vehemently inveighed against his son that he caused him to hang himself. The like story is written of Archilochus and Licambes.
Tirtaeus The Lacedemonians being enemies to the Messenians, through Apollo's counsel required a captain of the men of Athens. The Athenians as it were disdaining the Lacedemonians gave them for a captain this Tirtaeus a poet being lame and impotent, under whose ensign they lost three notable battles, wherewith being discouraged, they intended never more to fight, and fled homewards, had not Tirtaeus stayed them, who reciting certain verses that he made, so enflamed the hearts of his soldiers, that life with them was nothing regarded, but all their care and thought was for their burial, whereupon tying certain things to their arms, whereby they after death be known, they marched forward, and discomfited their enemies.

51–3 *Plato ... De Furore Poetico*: Plato's brief dialogue *Ion* examines the nature of divine inspiration in poetry and eloquence.
80 *knowledgement*: formal acknowledgement; legal cognizance. OED gives three examples, all from legal writings of the first half of the seventeenth century. Possibly the reading should be 'acknowledgement' rather than 'a knowledgement.'
86 *Zoilus*: 'A malicious poet, that wrote a book of railing verses against the noble works of Homer, and therefore is called Homeromastix, that is, Homer's scourge ... Of him, all malicious carpers of other men's works be called Zoili' (Cooper).

Textual Appendix

Of the five copies known to exist of Googe's *Eclogues, Epitaphs, and Sonnets* of 1563 (STC 12048), only that in the Huntington Library (31415) contains the complete text. This copy is available on University Microfilms (Reel 344), and in a 'facsimile' reprint published in 1968. The latter has been silently altered in various places and is not a reliable guide. The 1563 volume was not reprinted until Edward Arber's edition of 1871, which is based on the copy now in the British Library, but is not entirely accurate. There are no known surviving manuscripts. The Huntington Library copy, hereafter referred to as H, is taken as the copy-text of this edition. Its description is as follows:

Title-page Eglogs | *Epytaphes,* and *Sonettes.* | Newly written by | *Barnabe Googe*: | 1563. | 15. Marche. | ℂ Imprinted at London, by | Thomas Colwell, for Raffe | Newbery, dwelyng in | Fleetstrete a little a= | boue the Conduit | in the late shop | of Thomas | Bartelet.

Colophon ℂ Imprinted at London | in S. Brydes Churchyarde, | by *Thomas ColWell,* for | *Raufe Nevvbery.* | And are to be sold at his shop | in Fleetestrete, a lytle aboue the Conduit. | 1563. | 15 *Die Mensis March.* | [Ornament]

Collation 8°, 140 × 90mm, (type-page 93 × 65). A(or a)^8 b(or B)^3 A–B^8 C^8+ additional leaf c.iii. D^4 E–K^8 [$5(-A(or a)1, A(or a)4, D4, F4, H4, J4; A(or a)3 mis-signed A.u.) signed roman numerals. $1 are signed with numeral], 88 leaves, leaf 88 blank. Types: various sizes of black letter, with italics as a subsidiary fount.

Contents A(or a)1: title (verso blank); A(or a)2–A(or a)4: commendatory verses; A(or a)4^v: arms of B. Googe; A(or a)5–A(or a)7: dedication; A(or a)7^v: woodcut; A(or a)8–b(or B)1^v: 'L. Blundeston to the Reader'; b(or B)2–b(or B)3^v: 'The Preface of L. Blundeston' (no CW b(or B)3^v); A1–D4^v: Eclogues (C3^v blank; no CW D4^v); E1–E5: Epitaphs; E5–H6^v: Sonnets (CW wrong F8^v); H6^v–K6^v:

Cupido Conquered; K7: Colophon with small bird and flower border piece; $K7^v$: Faults escaped; K8 blank.

The volume is bound in handsome brown gilt-tooled leather (Russia), with the gilt monogram G.S. back and front. 'G.S.' is George Steevens, the noted eighteenth-century Shakespearian scholar and collector. (For information about his achievements, his quarrels with other great scholars and collectors such as Capell and Malone, his friendship with Johnson, and the disposition of his library, see *DNB*.) Steevens has made a few notes on a flyleaf, including the comment 'There is no scarcer book in the English Language than these Eglogs &c. Dr Farmer, Mr T. Warton, & Mr Reed have never met with them.' The volume was obtained for Henry E. Huntington at the sale of 8 February 1922 of the Britwell Court library.

The other four copies are as follows:

B British Library. Huth 35.
This copy differs from H in having a blank leaf at the end of the preliminary material (b(or B)4), and in lacking c3 and K8. There is an interesting shadow impression on the blank verso of C3 (see discussion below). The copy is described and commented upon by A.W. Pollard *Catalogue of the Fifty Manuscripts and Printed Books Bequeathed to the British Museum by Alfred H. Huth* (London 1912) 59–60.

C Trinity College, Cambridge. Capell $*19^2$.
Bound following Shakespeare's *Lucrece* (1598). Lacks C3, K7, K8. The copy is described in *Capell's Shakespeariana: Catalogue of the books presented by Edward Capell to the library of Trinity College in Cambridge compiled by W.W. Greg M.A.* (Cambridge 1903) p 48.

T Owned by Robert H. Taylor, deposited in the Princeton University Library.
Bound following Googe's Palingenius (1561). Spine: 'Works of Barnabe Googe.' Lacks c3, C4, C5, but has blank leaf b(or B)4, as in B. A(or a)2–7 are misbound before the title-page.

J Owned by Dr B. Juel-Jensen, Oxford.
Lacks A(or a), b(or B), A, B1–6, I8, K. Copy begins B7 and ends $I7^v$, and contains both C3 and c3. There is a shadow image on the blank verso of C3, as in B.

The volume was entered in the Stationers' Register in the period 22 July 1562–22 July 1563. The entry as transcribed by Arber reads 'Recevyd of Raufe newbery for his lycense for pryntinge of a *Certayne egloges Ephitaphes and*

Sonattes wryten by BARNABE GOOGE ... vj^{d}'(1:208). It is probably mere coincidence that Neville's translation of Seneca's *Oedipus* is entered to Thomas Colwell only four items later, but the fact that Colwell served as printer in 1563 to both the cousins and friends is noteworthy.

Newbery's earlier connections with Googe seem a good deal more than coincidental. In 1563 Newbery was at the beginning of what was to be a long and distinguished career.[1] He had been made a freeman of the Stationers' Company on 21 January 1560, but for the first five years of his career entries to do with him in the Register relate more often to fines and apprentices than to copyright. The first book entries are two together, falling (according to Arber 1:127) between 4 March and 4 May 1560; they are 'a boke Called *the popes usurped premace*' and a 'boke Called *PALLINGENIUS*.' The first of these is a translation by Thomas Gressop of Nilus Cabasilas's *Briefe Treatise of the Pope's vsurped Primacye* (STC 4325), and contains a dedicatory poem signed B.G., generally accepted as by Googe (see p 125, and Introduction). The second is the first instalment of Googe's translation of Palingenius's *Zodiake of Life* (STC 19148).[2] In the next five years the only works entered to Newbery besides Googe's *Eclogues* are a ballad, an 'accidence' in Latin and Irish, and an almanac. That he was struggling for custom at this time may also be indicated in his being among the nineteen members of the Company fined for selling an unauthorized edition of Nostradamus (Aldis 384). However, his copyright on the first three books of Palingenius extended to the rest of the translation, and he brought out 'The first syxe bokes' in 1561, and the complete twelve books by 18 April 1565. It is pleasant to suppose that Newbery's fortunes were founded on the popularity of Googe's work, by providing him with an attractive item to exchange with other publishers for copies of their books, in the manner of building up a stock in trade described by Aldis (388), but of course the Register does not provide a complete picture of transactions, particularly at this early period of the Company's incorporation.

Thomas Colwell, who printed the *Eclogues* for Newbery, was also made a freeman of the Company in 1560, on 30 August. He rapidly succeeded to the shop of Robert and Nicholas Wyer at the sign of St John the Evangelist at Charing Cross, where, 'using Wyer's old black-letter type, ornaments, and devices,' he 'continued the tradition of printing cheap and popular literature' (Hale 223). In 1562 Colwell moved his shop to St Bride's Churchyard, and then moved again to Fleet Street, beneath the Conduit.[3] At first glance Colwell is most notable as a printer of ballads, and he is the first named by Aldis as 'among the most active producers' of this form of sensational and sentimental popular literature (390), but further consideration of his output shows an interesting association with the attempt to make the classics accessible to the unlearned, and also suggests Protestant sympathies. His edition of Bale's *Three Laws* in 1562 may, as David Hale implies (224), be seen as a tribute to that vigorous polemicist,[4] and his edition of Neville's *Oedipus* in 1563 was followed by several other translations of Seneca's plays, as well as translations from Ovid and Horace. But Colwell's concern for the learning and religion of the age was not matched by a care for craftsmanship. The type and ornaments he had inherited were old, and as Hale notes (225), he made little attempt to replace them. The careless appearance of his work does not inspire much confidence in the authority of his orthography, punctuation, or disposition of the text, and does much to reconcile a modern editor to drastic modernization.

The needs and habits of printer and bookseller, and the physical makeup of the volume of the *Eclogues*, can help in determining whether the story told in the prefatory material of how and why the poems came to be published represents the facts, or whether it is an example of the fictions maintained in support of the convention of unwilling publication;[5] and may also cast light on when some of the poems were completed.

Googe was on the Continent from the autumn of 1561 until June 1562. Blundeston's address to the reader, in which he explains why he boldly hazarded the printing of the poems left (as we are told in his verse preface) in his care, is dated 27 May 1562. The hesitations, arguments, and literary activities that Googe describes in his dedication took place some time between June 1562 and 15 March 1563, the date on the colophon. Exactly how long after his own return to England Googe discovered that his poems were in the hands of the printer is not clear, since Googe speaks of Blundeston's 'absence from the city,' and 'his return of late.' Googe's utter amazement at the fate of his trifles seems to have permitted his accepting the argument that the matter 'being so far past, and paper provided for the impression thereof ... could not without great hindrance of the poor printer be now revoked.' At this stage of their careers both Colwell and Newbery might well be described as poor, and furthermore the point about the paper has more force than perhaps may be appreciated by modern readers (particularly those sitting in the middle of Canadian forests). Paper was expensive, scarce, and highly prized (Warkentin 434). That sheets had been gathered together from various sources for the printing of the *Eclogues* is suggested by the extraordinary diversity of watermarks discoverable in the surviving copies.[6] These considerations might increase acceptance of the sincerity of Googe's expressed reluctance to publish.

Having submitted to the arguments of Blundeston and allowed the publication to go forward, how much did Googe add to the 'paper bunch' of 'filèd work' of his 'flowing head,' and how closely involved was he with the setting up and printing of his work? In his dedication the only work he mentions having added to is 'Cupido Conquered,' 'the greater part whereof with little advice I lately ended.' However, the first and seventh eclogues, and the poem 'To the tune of Appelles,' are all drawn from Montemayor's *Diana*, which he could have seen in England (since there were as many as seven editions available between its first appearance in 1559 and the time that Googe left England in the latter part of 1561), but which he is much more likely to have encountered in Spain; and the three poems 'Going towards Spain' 'At Bonneval in France,' and 'Coming Homeward out of Spain,' while in one sense derived from Wyatt, are more reasonably seen as related to actual experience than as solely exercises in literary imitation.

Physically the work seems divided into four: *i* 11 (or 12) leaves, or 1½ sheets, of preliminary material; *ii* 28 (or 29) leaves, or 3½ sheets A–C^8, D^4, containing the eclogues; *iii* 16 leaves, or 2 sheets, E–F^8, containing the epitaphs and some sonnets; *iv* 32 (or 31) leaves, or 4 sheets, containing the rest of the sonnets and 'Cupido Conquered.' There is no catchword on b(or B)3^v, which occasions no surprise, since it was the usual (though not invariable) practice to set up the preliminary material after the text had been composed, and since b(or B)4 where it exists, is blank. The lack of a catchword on $D4^v$ is more significant, and suggests that D was set up after E. The catchword on $F8^v$ is wrong: '¶If' instead of '¶To.' ('If' is the first word of the poem, though not of the title, of the little sentence from Ovid which appears three poems later on G3.) One might guess that printing halted at this point to accommodate new material (the four short poems referred to above, and the completion of 'Cupido Conquered'), and that some rearrangement of the remaining sonnets was undertaken. The setting up of E and F seems to have been plain sailing: the running titles change accurately from Epitaphs to Sonnets, the poems are regularly spaced, there is only one change in the 'Faults escaped,' and (apart from an interesting cluster of press variants on the outer forme of F) there are few errors. The setting up of G to K seems to have been almost as straightforward, but there is some crowding of the poems on $G6^v$, the number of 'Faults escaped' rises sharply, the number of errors increases, and there is a small muddle in running titles at the change from 'Sonnets' to 'Cupido conquered': on H7 'Cupido' should read 'conquered' and on $H8^v$ 'conquered' should read 'Cupido' (7 and 8^v are of course next to one another in the forme). The situation in A–D is far from being so simple. A is relatively clean with catchwords and running titles all in place, and only the loss of the A in the signature of A4 (in two of four copies) of note. In B there is some confusion in running titles (B1 'quarta' for 'tertia'; B2 and B3 'tertia' for 'quarta'; $B6^v$ 'quinta' for 'Egloga'), but composition proceeds without a major hitch through the sixth eclogue, which begins at the top of $B7^v$ and concludes at the end of C3. The catchword on C3 is 'Egloga,' but $C3^v$ is blank. The seventh eclogue begins at the top of c3, continues on $c3^v$, and thence to C4, where the running title reads 'sexta' instead of 'septima.' It then proceeds normally to its conclusion on C7, where the catchword 'Egloga' leads to the beginning of the eighth eclogue on $C7^v$. The catchword from c3 to $c3^v$ is wrong ('Thus' instead of 'Thou').[7] The eighth eclogue runs from $C7^v$ to $D4^v$ with all running titles and catchwords correct. As already noted, $D4^v$ lacks a catchword. Apparently some problem with the copy led the printer to leave a blank page after setting up the sixth eclogue and continue setting up further on. Unfortunately one page was not enough, necessitating the printing and insertion of another leaf. In one copy at least (C) this leaf was mistakenly substituted for C3, and in another (B) the insertion was not made. It is puzzling that the printing of the forme went ahead with one page blank, but perhaps by that time it was realized that the omitted copy would require two pages, and therefore an additional leaf. The most reasonable explanation of this rather awkward bit of printing business seems to be that Googe wanted to rewrite the beginning of the seventh eclogue. Although in some ways the eclogue closely paraphrases Montemayor's *Diana*, Googe is clearly selecting and adding material to further his own artistic purposes. One other odd little circumstance perhaps indicates unusual confusion over this sheet: two of the surviving leaves C3, in (B) and (J), have on the blank verso a faint shadow image of a woodcut, about 9.3cm long × 6.8cm wide in a double rule frame.[8]

It seems, then, that the physical evidence of the book indicates that Googe was adding to, rewriting, and rearranging his poems while they were at press. The compositors embarked on the eclogues as the first work in the volume, but knowing that these poems were not quite ready, estimating that they would take more than three sheets, and having already run into a problem with C, laid them aside and began setting up the epitaphs on E. Possibly there was another break in the process when sheets E and F were completed, at which time Googe added and rearranged poems, and made some changes and corrections to the outer forme of F (see list of press-variant formes below, and notes on 'The Answer of L. Blundeston to the same,' 'To Alexander Neville,' and 'To M. Henry Cobham of the most blessed state of Life'). The preliminary material, together with D, was set last, and the final addition was the setting of the insert leaf c3.[9] The strong indications that the copy the printer had in his hands when he started setting up the work was unsatisfactory in several ways to Googe lead me to accept the substantial truth of the story outlined by him and Blundeston, rather than interpreting it 'as an example of the straits to which versifiers were driven to circumvent the 16th-century convention that a gentleman's poems should be circulated in manuscript, not committed to print' (Pollard *Catalogue* 60).

VARIANTS AND EMENDATIONS

Apart from the process of modernization described in the Note on the Text following the Introduction, and the silent correction of broken letters, the changes to the text are of three kinds: press-variants, faults escaped, and editorial emendations. In the following list of alterations to the text each copy is denoted as in the descriptive list above in identifying press-variants; faults escaped are identified FE. Emendations made by previous editors, Arber and Stephens, are so identified;[10] other editorial emendations are identified Ed. The unemended readings on the right are given in old spelling, with only long s modernized, but italicization is ignored.

*1.55 Unto Ed] Vnto to
7.9 Amongst Arber] Amonst
7.24 heavens Arber] heaues
8.7 secret Arber] sccrete
8.113 (margin) Pale. Arber] omitted
9. (throughout) Egon FE] Agon
9.111 Faustus Arber] Fanstus
10. (speakers) Faustus Arber] Faustns
10.179 Calisto FE] Calicto
11.9 Diana FE] Duerda
11.32 mischiefs Ed] mysciefes
11.82 Silvan FE] Siluanus
11.101 Diana's FE] Guerdas
11.115 Selvagia FE] Seluagina
11.122 women Arber] womens
12.89 (margin) Daniel Ed] Dauid (Arber adds ?Daniel)
12.186 slaves BCJT] saues H
12.257 Eglogae BCJT] Egluge H
13.12 slain Arber] slayue
14.14 sure FE] soore
16.6 The pleasant Arber, Stephens] Tht pelasaunt
16.26 takes Ed] take
19.23 appears Stephens] appeare
24 (title) State Arber, Stephens] Sate
25.25 thou Arber, Stephens] thon
31.7 drive Stephens] dryne
32.25–32 Thou livest ... case FE] omitted

34.10 plaints Ed] playn
35.10 the Arber, Stephens] tthe
41.6 strangers Arber, Stephens] staungers
43.13 do pinch Arber, Stephens] do= (pych
45.6 governance Arber, Stephens] goueruaunce
45.8 on FE] in
*46a.8 for FE] fo
*46a.9 cruelly FE] Crueltie
47.24 thee, alas Stephens] the I alas
48.110 every Arber] enery
48.343 shining Arber] shynyg
48.585 Three Ed] thie
48.604 horses FE] hores
48.713 turning Arber] turyng
48.721 misfortune Arber] misfortuue
48.760–1 at. / I saw Arber] at. / that late I wondred at, / I sawe (Line 760, which occurs at the end of K6, is repeated at the top of K6^{v}, although the catchword on K6 is correct).

PRESS-VARIANT FORMES

A(or a) Outer forme
Corrected H; uncorrected BCT
8^{v} fynde the thankfull] fynd the vnthankfull
A(or a) Inner forme
Corrected HB; uncorrected CT
8 reading the] reding this
b(or B) Outer forme
Corrected BHT; uncorrected C
2^{v} gesse] gerse
past] part
Pyrenei] Pryanei
3 Esops] Isops
A Inner forme
Corrected BT; uncorrected CH
1^{v} growe,] growe
in tyme,] in, tyme,
4sig A.iiii] .iiii.
C Outer forme
Corrected H; uncorrected CJ (B shaved).
4^{v}margin Siluan.] Silanu.

D Outer forme

Corrected BCJT; uncorrected H

3 Slaues] Saues

4^v Egloge] Egluge

D Inner forme

Corrected BCJ; uncorrected HT

1^v yet in] ye tin

F Outer forme

Corrected CHJT; uncorrected B

2^v breede] breedes

and hap= / pye] and / happye

3 hym synge] hym to synge

5 I well do mynde,] Remembrest thou?

G Outer forme

Corrected CHT; uncorrected BJ

8^v house] hou e

G Inner forme

Corrected H; uncorrected BCJT

8 time] time,

I Inner forme

Corrected CHJT; uncorrected B

1^v quoth] quo h

Only some of the above formes can confidently be described as in corrected and uncorrected states: A(or a) Outer, b(or B) Inner, D Outer, F Outer, and possibly A(or a) Inner and C Outer. The variants on A Inner, D Inner, G Outer and Inner, and I inner can all be explained by slipped type or dropped letters, and the incorrect state is probably the second state. Colwell's type includes many broken or worn letters and sometimes they take the ink unevenly.

A NOTE ON THE WOODCUTS

The woodcut of Googe's arms is the same as that used in the 1560 edition of the first three books of Palingenius, printed by John Tisdale for Newbery, but in that volume there is a two-line Latin motto below the woodcut instead of the simple name 'B. Googe.' (Googe's arms do not appear in the 1561 Palingenius, but increasingly elaborated versions appear in the 1565 and 1576 editions.)

The woodcut of two figures, identified above as Daphnes and Amintas, is strangely placed on A(or a)7^v before Blundeston's address and preface, instead of immediately before the first eclogue, which it is evidently intended to embellish. (In the present edition both woodcuts have been repositioned.) It is a factotum block, derived from the *Kalendar of Shepherds*. A very similar block may be seen on p 149 of G.C. Heseltine's 1931 modernized edition of *The Kalendar and Compost of Shepherds*. Heseltine apparently reproduces this woodcut from the 1493 French edition of G. Marchant (British Library G.10535), since it does not appear in the Julian Notary English edition of ?1518 (British Library C71 f 2; STC 22410) which forms the text of his edition. Colwell's woodcut, without the names, appears on the verso of the title-page of one of the British Library's copies (C.31.a.27) of the *Treasure of Poor Men* (STC 24206a). The ubiquity of these woodcuts is described by Edward Hodnett: 'Throughout the first half of the sixteenth century English printers made use of factotum blocks – small figures of men and women, trees, and buildings, usually borderless – which they sprinkled over the pages of their books. Often a ribbon above them contains a printed legend, as of the character represented. The well-spring of these cuts, as Dr Pollard has pointed out, is Vérard's *Terence*. They seem to have entered England in 1506, when Pynson acquired Vérard's *Kalendar of Shepherds* blocks for his own edition, though an earlier occurrence is possible. Vérard's habit of repeating these stock figures several times in the same book appealed to Pynson, de Worde, and their fellows, and they copied the figures as avidly as a provincial milliner copies a metropolitan style. Then, finding them increasingly useful and economical, they copied their own copies. As a result, so many of these cuts exist and differ so minutely from one another that they cannot be identified by verbal description, and since nothing short of the reproduction of every one would be useful, they have not been included in the Catalogue' (vii–viii).

Notes

1 Junior Warden of the Stationers' Company for two terms (1583–4; 1584–5), Senior Warden for two terms (1589–90; 1590–1), and Master for two terms (1598; 1601). He was involved in such major publishing enterprises as Hakluyt's *Voyages*, Holinshed's *Chronicles*, the Bible and the Book of Common Prayer, and Stow's *Annals*. He apparently retired in 1605, and died in 1607. If he was at least twenty-four when made a freeman (cf Aldis 388), he was probably born c1535. (*DNB* 14:314; McKerrow 199; Bennett 65, 297).

2 The Cabasilas was printed for Newbery by Henry Sutton, and the colophon is dated 'In the yere of our Lorde a thousande fyue hundred & sixty. The .xvi. daye of Marche.' The Palingenius was printed for Newbery by John Tisdale; the title-page and colophon give the year only, but the English dedication to Lady Hales is dated 'From Staple Inne at London the eighte and twenty of march,' and the Latin dedication to a group of fellow students is dated 'Decimo Martii Anno Christi. 1560 aetatis nostrae .xx.'

3 Hale says (224) that Googe's *Eclogues* was the first book printed by Colwell after moving to Fleet Street, but the colophon clearly states that it was printed in St Bride's Churchyard, and the title-page of Neville's *Oedipus* informs us that Colwell was still printing in St Bride's Churchyard on 28 April 1563.

4 However, Hale must be mistaken in suggesting the tribute was 'on the occasion of his death,' since Bale died in November 1563.

5 See Bennett *English Books and Readers 1475–1557* especially chapter 2, and *English Books and Readers 1558–1603*, especially chapter 1. Routine protestations of unwillingness to publish come mainly from the last quarter of the century.

6 In the Huntington copy, of the eleven (or ten and two half) sheets, I could find no watermarks on two, and on the remaining nine sheets there are five different watermarks. One could be Briquet *Main* 11464, but this is paper of a very early date (1498); another could be Briquet *Pot* 12748

(1544) or 12790 (1544) or 12798 (1555); another is close to Briquet *Sphère* 13998 (1553). At least nine other different watermarks are discoverable in the remaining four copies. (See Briquet *Les Filigranes*.)

7 'Thus' is the right catchword for $D3^{r-v}$, but I cannot see how this would have any significance.

8 I have not been able to find a suitable candidate for this shadow image in books printed by Colwell in this period that I have been able to examine.

9 It is tempting to speculate that b(or B) and D were set together, and that after a few sheets had been printed, the insert was set up in the blank spaces for b(or B)4, as in the diagram on the following page.

10 It should be noted that Stephens provides a modernized reprint rather than an edition: emendations are not recorded, and not all faults escaped have been incorporated.

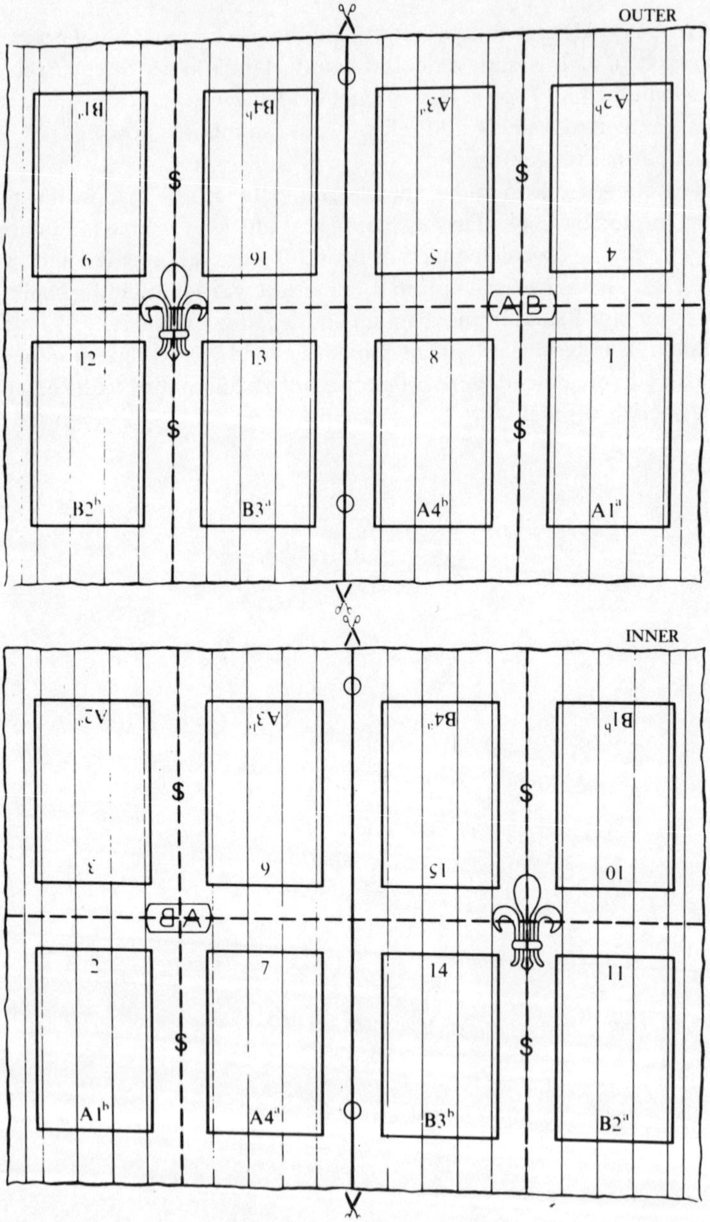

Diagram from Philip Gaskell *A New Introduction to Bibliography* (New York and Oxford: Oxford University Press 1972) 94

Works Cited

Abbott, E.A. *A Shakespearian Grammar*. 1869; rpt London 1894

Academiae Cantabrigiensis lachrymae … tumulo … D. Philippi Sidneij sacratae per A. Nevillum. London 1587

Aesop. *Fables in Englysshe with all his lyfe*. London 1551

Aldis, H.G. 'The Book-Trade, 1557–1625.' In *Cambridge History of English Literature* ed A.W. Ward and A.R. Waller, 4:378–414. Cambridge 1950

Alsop, J.D. 'The Dramatis Personae in Barnabe Googe's Critique of the Marian Persecution.' *Notes and Queries* ns 28 (1981) 512–15

—'The Sixth Eclogue of Baptista Mantuan and the Elizabethan Poet Barnabe Googe.' *Cahiers Elizabéthains*, 25 (1984) 1–8

Aratus. *Phaenomena*. Trans G.R. Mair. In *Callimachus and Lycophron*, trans A.W. Mair and G.R. Mair. Loeb Classical Library. London and Cambridge, Mass 1921

—*The Aratus Ascribed to Germanicus Caesar*. Ed D.B. Gain. London 1976

Arber, Edward. *A Transcript of the Stationers' Registers: 1554–1640*. 5 vols. 1875–94; rpt New York 1950

Ariosto, L. *Ludovico Ariosto's Orlando Furioso Translated into English Heroical Verse by Sir John Harington (1591)*. Ed Robert McNulty. Oxford 1972

Ascham, Roger. *The Schoolmaster*. Ed Lawrence V. Ryan. Charlottesville, Virginia 1974

Authores poetae morales octo. Leyden 1540

Baldwin, T.W. *William Shakespere's Small Latine and Lesse Greeke*. 2 vols. Urbana 1944

Balista, Christopher [Arbaleste, Christophe]. *The overthrow of the gout, written in Latin verse*. [Tr … by B.G., ie Barnabe Googe?] London 1577

Barnett, Richard C. *Place, Profit, and Power: A Study of the Servants of William Cecil, Elizabethan Statesman*. Chapel Hill 1969

Barrell, John and John Bull, eds. *A Book of English Pastoral Verse*. New York 1975

Bartholomaeus Anglicus. *Batman uppon Bartholome his booke De proprietatibus rerum (1582)*. Facsimile reprint with Introduction and Index by J. Schäfer. Hildesheim and New York 1976

Beckingsale, Bernard W. *Burghley: Tudor Statesman, 1520–1598*. New York 1967

Bennett, H.S. *English Books and Readers 1475–1557*. Cambridge 1952

—*English Books and Readers 1558–1603*. Cambridge 1965

Bennett, J.A.W. 'The Early Fame of Gavin Douglas's Eneados.' *MLN* 61 (1946) 83–8

Bertholdus, Andreas. *The Wonderfull and strange effect and vertues of a new Terra sigillata*. Trans B.G. London 1587

Beza, Theodore. *Poemata*. Paris 1548

Bible. *The Geneva Bible, 1560*. Facsimile reprint ed Lloyd E. Berry. Madison 1969

Black, J.B. *The Reign of Elizabeth*. Oxford 1952

The Book of Common Prayer 1559. Ed John E. Booty. Charlottesville, Virginia 1976

Bradner, Leicester. *The Life and Poems of Richard Edwards*. New Haven and London 1927

Briquet, Charles M. *Les Filigranes*. 4 vols. 2nd ed, Leipzig 1923

Brown, Carleton. *Religious Lyrics of the XIVth Century*. 2nd ed, rev G.V. Smithers, Oxford 1952

Brydges, Sir Samuel Egerton. *The British Bibliographer*. 4 vols. London 1810–14

—*Restituta*. 4 vols. London 1814–16

Cabasilas, Nilus. *A Briefe Treatise ... of the Pope's usurped Primacye*. Trans T. Gressop. London 1560

Campbell, Lily B. See *The Mirror for Magistrates*.

Castiglione, Baldassare. *The Courtier*. Trans Sir Thomas Hoby. Everyman's Library. London 1928

Chaloner, Sir Thomas. *De republica anglorum*. London 1579

Chambers, R. *The Book of Days: A Miscellany of Popular Antiquities*. 2 vols. London 1863

Chaucer, G. *The Works of Geoffrey Chaucer*. Ed F.N. Robinson. 2nd ed, Cambridge, Mass 1957

—*The Works, 1532*. Menston, Yorkshire 1969

Cicero. *The worthye booke of old age otherwyse entituled the elder Cato, now englished*. Trans T[homas] Newton. London 1569

—*Foure severall treatises: conteyninge discourses of Frendshippe, old age, paradoxes and Scipio his dreame*. Trans T[homas] Newton. London 1577

—*The Letters to His Friends*. Trans W. Glynn Williams. Loeb Classical Library. 3 vols. London and Cambridge, Mass 1927–9

Clark, Peter. *English Provincial Society*. Sussex 1977

Conley, C.H. *The First English Translators of the Classics*. 1927. Rpt Port Washington, NY 1967

Cook, Timothy. 'Who were Barnabe Googe's Two Coridons?' *Notes and Queries* ns 24 (1977) 497–9

Cooper, Helen. *Pastoral: Medieval into Renaissance*. Totowa, New Jersey 1977 [cited H. Cooper]

Cooper, Thomas. *Thesaurus Linguae Romanae et Britannicae 1565*. A Scolar Press Facsimile. Menston, England 1969 [cited Cooper]

Corrozet, Gilles. *Les divers propos memorables des nobles et illustres hommes de la Chrestienté*. Paris 1556

—*Memorable Conceits of divers noble and famous personages of Christendome*. London 1602

Crinò. See Spenser *The Shepheardes Calender*.

Cuningham, William. *The Cosmographical Glasse*. London 1559

Diana. See Montemayor.

Dickens, A.G. *The English Reformation*. London 1970

Dictionary of National Biography. Ed Leslie Stephen and Sidney Lee. 63 vols. London 1885–1900 [cited DNB]

Douthwaite, William Ralph. *Gray's Inn: Its History and Associations*. London 1886

Du Bartas, Guillaume de Saluste, Sieur. *The Divine Weeks and Works*. Trans Joshua Sylvester. Ed Susan Snyder. 2 vols. Oxford 1979.

Eccles, Mark. 'Barnabe Googe in England, Spain, and Ireland.' *English Literary Renaissance* 15 (1985) 353–70

Edwards, Richard. See *The Paradise of Dainty Devices*.

Elyot, Sir Thomas. *The Governor*. Everyman's Library. London 1907

Erasmus, Desiderius. *Proverbes or adagies ... gathered ... by Richard Taverner*. London 1539

—*Apophthegms*. Trans Nicholas Udall. London 1542

Fairfield, Leslie P. *John Bale Mythmaker for the English Reformation*. West Lafayette, Indiana 1976

Fieler. See Googe.

FQ. See Spenser *The Faerie Queene*.

Fowler, Alastair. *Kinds of Literature: An Introduction to the Theory of Genres and Modes*. Cambridge, Mass 1982

Garcilaso de la Vega. *The Works of Garcilasso de la Vega* ... translated ... by J.H. Wiffen. London 1823

Gascoigne, George. *The Posies*. Ed J.W. Cunliffe. Cambridge 1907

Gaskell, Philip. *A New Introduction to Bibliography*. New York and Oxford 1972

Googe, Barnabe. *Eglogs, Epytaphes, and Sonettes (1563)*. A facsimile reproduction with Introduction by F.B. Fieler. Gainsville, Florida 1968

—Ed Edward Arber. English Reprints. London 1871
—*A newe Booke called the Shippe of safegarde*. London 1569
—'A Table briefly declaring the signification and meaning of all such Poetical words as are contained within this book, for the better understanding thereof.' In *The firste syxe bokes of ... Palingenius, called the Zodiake of life*. London 1561
—*Selected Poems of Barnabe Googe*. Ed Alan Stephens. Denver 1961 [cited Stephens]
A Gorgeous Gallery of Gallant Inventions (1578). Ed Hyder E. Rollins. Cambridge, Mass 1926
Grafton, Richard. *A Chronicle ... of Englande ... from the Creation of the worlde, unto ... the reigne of ... Queene Elizabeth*. London 1569
Green, Richard Firth. *Poets and Princepleasers: Literature and the English Court in the Late Middle Ages*. Toronto 1980
Greenlaw, Edwin A. '*The Shepheards Calender*.' PMLA 26 (1911) 419–51
Greg, Walter W. *Pastoral Poetry and Pastoral Drama*. London 1906
Guiney, Louise Imogen, ed. *Recusant Poets: With a Selection from their Work*. Vol 1: *Saint Thomas More to Ben Jonson*. London 1938
Hale, David G. 'Thomas Colwell: Elizabethan Printer.' *The Library* 5th ser 19 (1964) 223–6
A Handful of Pleasant Delights (1584). Ed Hyder E. Rollins. New York 1965
Hankins, John Erskine. 'The Poems of George Turbervile Edited with Critical Notes and a Study of his Life and Works.' PhD Dissertation. Yale University 1929
Harrison, T.P., Jr. 'Googe's *Eglogs* and Montemayor's *Diana*.' *University of Texas Studies in English* 5 (1925) 68–78
Harvey, G. *The Works of Gabriel Harvey*. Ed A.B. Grosart. 3 vols. 1884; rpt. New York 1966
—*Gabriel Harvey's Marginalia*. Ed G.C. Moore-Smith. Stratford-upon-Avon 1913
Hasted, Edward. *The History and Topographical Survey of the County of Kent*. 12 vols. 2nd ed 1797–1801; rpt Wakefield, Yorkshire 1972
Henkel, Arthur and Albrecht Schöne. *Emblemata*. Stuttgart 1976
Herbert, J.A., ed. *Catalogue of Romances in the Department of Manuscripts in the British Museum*. Vol 3. London 1910
Heresbach, Conrad. *Foure Bookes of Husbandry Translated by Barnabe Googe (1577)*. The English Experience 323. Amsterdam 1971
Heywood, J. *Jasper Heywood and His Translations of Seneca's Troas, Thyestes and Hercules Furens*. Ed H. de Vocht. 1913; rpt Vaduz 1963
Hodnett, Edward. *English Woodcuts 1480–1535*. 1935; rpt with additions and corrections, Oxford 1973

Holinshed, Raphael. *Holinshed's Chronicles of England, Scotland, and Ireland*. 6 vols. 1807–8; rpt New York 1965
Homer. *Ten Books of Homers Iliades translated out of French by Arthur Hall*. London 1581
Horace. *The Odes and Epodes*. Trans C.E. Bennett. Loeb Classical Library. London and New York 1914
Howell, T. *The Poems of Thomas Howell*. Ed A.B. Grosart. Manchester 1879
Hudson, Hoyt H. 'Sonnets by Barnabe Googe.' *PMLA* 48 (1933) 293–4
Hunt, Clay. 'The Elizabethan Background of Neo-Classic Polite Verse.' *ELH* 8 (1941) 273–304
Hunter, G.K. 'Drab and Golden Lyrics of the Renaissance.' In *Forms of Lyric: Selected Papers from the English Institute* ed R.A. Brower, pp 1–18. New York 1970
Huth, Alfred H. *Ancient Ballads and Broadsides*. London 1867
Jones, Richard F. *The Triumph of the English Language*. Stanford 1953
The Kalender & Compost of Shepherds. Ed G.C. Heseltine. London 1930
Kirchmeyer, Thomas. *The Popish Kingdome, or reigne of Antichrist englyshed by Barnabe Googe*. London 1570
—Ed R.C. Hope. London 1880
Kolve, V.A. *Chaucer and the Imagery of Narrative: The First Five Canterbury Tales*. Stanford 1984
Lagnerius, Petrus. *M. Tull. Ciceronis sententiae illustriores, Apophthegmata* ... Lyon 1547
Lambarde, William. *A Perambulation of Kent*. With an introduction by Richard Church. Bath 1970
Langius, Josephus. *Polyanthea*. Frankfurt 1613
La Perrière, Guillaume de. *Le Theatre des Bons Engins*. Paris 1539
Lemprière, J. *Lemprière's Classical Dictionary of Proper Names Mentioned in Classical Authors Writ Large*. 1788; 3rd ed, introduction by R. Willetts, London 1984
Lewis, C.S. *English Literature in the Sixteenth Century Excluding Drama*. Oxford 1954
Lilly, Joseph. *Black-Letter Ballads and Broadsides*. London 1867
Lopez de Mendoza, Inigo, Marqués de Santillana. *The Proverbes*. Trans B. Googe. London 1579
Lopez Estrada, Francisco. See Montemayor.
Lycosthenes, Conrad. *Apophthegmata*. Cologne 1618
MacCaffrey, Wallace T. *The Shaping of the Elizabethan Regime*. Princeton, NJ 1968
McConica, James K. *English Humanists and Reformation Politics under Henry VIII and Edward VI*. Oxford 1965

McKerrow, Ronald B. *A Dictionary of Printers and Booksellers*. London 1910
McKisack, May. *Medieval History in the Tudor Age*. Oxford 1971
Major, Georg. *Sententiae veterum poetarum*. Paris 1551
Mantuan. *The Eclogues of Baptista Mantuanus*. Ed W.P. Mustard. Baltimore 1911
—*The eglogs ... turned into English verse, by G. Turbervile*. London 1567
Marlowe, Christopher. *The Complete Plays*. Ed J.B. Steane. Harmondsworth, Middlesex 1969
Marot, Clément. *Ladolescence clementine. Autrement, Les Oeuvres de Clement Marot*. Paris 1532
—Ed. V.L. Saulnier. Paris 1958
Martial. *Epigrams*. Trans Walter C.A. Ker. Loeb Classical Library. 2 vols. London and Cambridge, Mass 1919–20
Meier, G. See Major.
Merrill, L.R. 'Nicholas Grimald, the Judas of the Reformation.' PMLA 37 (1922) 216–27
Mills, Laurens J. *One Soul in Bodies Twain: Friendship in Tudor Literature and Stuart Drama*. Bloomington, Indiana 1937
Mirandula, Octavianus. *Illustrium poetarum flores*. Lyon 1553
The Mirror for Magistrates. Ed Lily B. Campbell. 1938; rpt New York 1960
Montemayor, Jorge de. *Los siete libros de la Diana*. Ed Francisco Lopez Estrada. Madrid 1954 [cited Lopez Estrada]
—*A Critical Edition of Yong's Translation of George of Montemayor's Diana and Gil Polo's Enamoured Diana*. Ed Judith M. Kennedy. Oxford 1968 [cited *Diana*]
Morey, Adrian. *The Catholic Subjects of Elizabeth I*. London 1978
Murrin, Michael J. 'Mantuan and the English Eclogue.' PhD Dissertation. Yale University 1965
Naogeorgus, Thomas. See Kirchmeyer.
Neville, Alexander. *A Nevylli Angli de furoribus Norfolciensium Ketto duce*. London 1575
—*Norfolkes furies: or a view of Ketts campe*. Trans R. W[oods]. London 1615
—See also *Academiae Cantabrigiensis ...*
Ovid. *The Art of Love and Other Poems*. Trans J.H. Mosley. Loeb Classical Library. London and Cambridge, Mass 1939
—*Fasti*. Trans Sir James George Frazer. Loeb Classical Library. London and Cambridge, Mass 1931
—*Heroides and Amores*. Trans Grant Showerman. Loeb Classical Library. London and Cambridge, Mass 1914
—*Metamorphoses*. Trans F.J. Miller. 2 vols. Vol 1 rev G.P. Goold. Loeb Classical Library. London and Cambridge, Mass 1977

—*Ovid's Metamorphoses: The Arthur Golding Translation 1567*. Ed John Frederick Nims. New York 1965.

—*Tristia. Ex Ponto*. Trans A.L. Wheeler. Loeb Classical Library. London and Cambridge, Mass 1924

The Oxford Dictionary of English Proverbs. 3rd ed rev F.P. Wilson. Oxford 1970 [cited *ODEP*]

The Oxford English Dictionary. A Corrected Re-Issue, and Supplements. Oxford 1933–86 [cited *OED*]

Palingenius, Marcellus. *The first syxe bokes of ... Palingenius, called the zodiake of life*. Trans B. Googe. London 1561

—*The Zodiake of Life: Translated by Barnabe Googe*. With an introduction by Rosemond Tuve. Delmar, NY 1976 [Cited Palingenius]

Panofsky, Edwin. *Studies in Iconology: Humanistic Themes in the Art of the Renaissance*. 1939; rpt New York 1962 [cited E. Panofsky]

Panofsky, Richard J. 'A Descriptive Study of English Mid-Tudor Short Poetry, 1557–1577.' PhD Dissertation. University of California, Santa Barbara 1975

Paradin, Claude. *Devises*. Lyon 1557

—*Heroicall Devises*. Trans P. S. London 1591

Parnell, Paul E. 'Barnabe Googe: A Puritan in Arcadia.' *Journal of English and Germanic Philology* 60 (1961) 273–81

The Paradise of Dainty Devices (1576). Ed H.E. Rollins. Cambridge, Mass 1927

Pattison, Bruce. *Music and Poetry of the English Renaissance*. London 1970

The Penguin Book of English Pastoral Verse. See Barrell and Bull.

Peirce, Brooke. 'Barnabe Googe: Poet and Translator.' PhD Dissertation, Harvard University 1954

Peterson, Douglas L. *The English Lyric from Wyatt to Donne*. Princeton 1967

Petrarch. *Sonnets and Songs*. Trans Anna Maria Armi. Introduction by Theodor E. Mommsen. New York 1968

—*The tryumphes*. Trans H. Parker, Lord Morley. London ?1555

Phaer, Thomas. See Virgil.

Pinkerton, William. 'Barnaby Googe.' *Notes & Queries* 3rd ser 3 (1863) 141–3, 181–4, 241–3, 301–2, 361–2

Plato. *The Dialogues of Plato*. Trans Benjamin Jowett. 5 vols. 3rd ed, New York and London 1892

Pliny. *Natural History*. Trans H. Rackham, W.H.S. Jones, and D.E. Eichholz. Loeb Classical Library. 10 vols. London and Cambridge, Mass 1938–63

Pollard, Alfred W. *Catalogue of the Fifty Manuscripts and Printed Books Bequeathed to the British Museum by Alfred H. Huth*. London 1912

—and G.R. Redgrave. *A Short-Title Catalogue of Books Printed in England, Scotland, & Ireland* ... 2nd ed, rev and enlarged by W.A. Jackson and F.S. Ferguson, completed by Katharine F. Pantzer. 2 vols. London 1976–86

Pound, Ezra. *Literary Essays of Ezra Pound*. Ed T.S. Eliot. London 1954

Prescott, Anne Lake. *French Poets and the English Renaissance: Studies in Fame and Translation*. New Haven 1978

Prest, Wilfrid R. *The Inns of Court under Elizabeth I and the Early Stuarts 1590–1640*. London 1972

Prouty, Charles T. *George Gascoigne*. 1942; rpt New York 1966

Puttenham, George. *The Arte of English Poesie*. Ed G.D. Willcock and A. Walker. Cambridge 1936

Read, Conyers. *Mr. Secretary Cecil and Queen Elizabeth*. London 1955

Riche, Barnabe. *Allarme to England*. London 1578

Robinson, Richard. *The rewarde of Wickednesse*. [London 1574]

Rollins, Hyder E. *An Analytical Index to the Ballad-entries (1557–1709) in the Register of the Company of Stationers of London*. 1924; rpt Hatboro, Pa 1967

Rollins, Hyder E. and Herschel Baker. *The Renaissance in England*. Boston 1954

Rosenberg, Eleanor. *Leicester Patron of Letters*. New York 1955

Rowland, Beryl. *Blind Beasts: Chaucer's Animal World*. Kent, Ohio 1971

Rubel, Veré L. *Poetic Diction in the English Renaissance*. 1941; rpt New York 1966

Saintsbury, George. *A History of English Prosody*. London 1923

Schuler, Robert M. 'Three Renaissance Scientific Poems.' *Studies in Philology* 75 no 5 (1978) 67–107

—'Theory and Criticism of the Scientific Poem in Elizabethan England.' *English Literary Renaissance* 15 (1985) 3–41

Seneca. *The lamentable tragedie of Oedipus ... out of Seneca. By Alexander Nevyle*. London 1563

—*Seneca His Tenne Tragedies. Translated into English. Ed. Thomas Newton Anno 1581*. With an introduction by T.S. Eliot. 1927; rpt Bloomington, Indiana 1966

—*Tragedies*. Trans F.J. Miller. Loeb Classical Library. 2 vols. London and Cambridge, Mass 1917

Shakespeare, William. *The Complete Works of Shakespeare*. Ed David M. Bevington. 3rd ed, Glenview, Illinois 1980

Sheidley, William E. *Barnabe Googe*. Twayne's English Authors Series. Boston 1981

—'A Timely Anachronism: Tradition and Theme in Barnabe Googe's "Cupido Conquered."' *Studies in Philology* 69 (1972) 150–66

Sidney, Sir Philip. *The Poems of Sir Philip Sidney*. Ed W.A. Ringler, Jr. Oxford 1962

—*An Apology for Poetry*. Ed Geoffrey Shepherd. London 1965

Simpson, Claude M. *The British Broadside Ballad and its Music*. New Brunswick, NJ 1966

Skeat, W.W., ed. *Chaucerian and Other Pieces: Supplement to the Works of Geoffrey Chaucer*. 1897; rpt Oxford 1963

Spearing, Evelyn M. 'Alexander Neville's Translation of Seneca's "Oedipus."' *Modern Language Review* 15 (1920) 359–63

Spenser, Edmund. *The Poetical Works of Edmund Spenser*. Ed J.C. Smith and E. de Sélincourt. London 1912

—*The Works of Edmund Spenser: A Variorum Edition*. Ed Edwin A. Greenlaw et al. 11 vols. Baltimore 1932–57

—*The Shepheardes Calender. Testo illustrato con le dodici xilografie originali*. Trans with an introduction and notes by Anna Maria Crinò. Florence 1950

—*The Faerie Queene*. Ed A.C. Hamilton. Longman Annotated English Poets. London 1977 [cited FQ]

Stern, Virginia F. *Gabriel Harvey; His Life, Marginalia and Library*. Oxford 1979

Stephens, Alan. See Googe.

Stevens, John. *Music and Poetry in the Early Tudor Court*. Cambridge 1979

Studley, John. *Studley's Translations of Seneca's Agamemnon and Medea*. Ed E.M. Spearing. 1913; rpt Vaduz 1963

Surrey, Henry Howard, Earl of. See *Tottel's Miscellany*.

Thompson, John. *The Founding of English Metre*. London 1961

Tilley, M.P. *A Dictionary of the Proverbs in England in the Sixteenth and Seventeenth Centuries*. Ann Arbor 1950

Tottel's Miscellany (1557–1587). Ed H.E. Rollins. 2 vols. 1928; rpt Cambridge, Mass 1966 [cited Tottel]

Trogus Pompeius. *Thabridgment of the histories of Trogus Pompeius, collected by Justine*. Trans A. Goldyng. London 1564

Tudor Tracts: 1532–1588. Intr. A.F. Pollard. London 1903

Turbervile, George. *Epitaphes, Epigrams, Songs and Sonets*. London 1567

—*Epitaphes, Epigrams, Songs and Sonets (1567) and Epitaphs and Sonnettes (1576)*. Facsimile reprint with an introduction by Richard J. Panofsky. Delmar, NY 1977

—See also Hankins.

Tuve, Rosemond. *Elizabethan and Metaphysical Imagery: Renaissance Poetic and Twentieth-Century Critics*. 1947; rpt Chicago 1961

Tydeman, William, ed. *English Poetry 1400–1580*. London 1970

Venn, John and J.A. Venn. *Alumni Cantabrigienses*. London 1922

Virgil. *The seven first bookes of the Eneidos converted in Englishe meter by T. Phaer*. London 1558 [and successive editions to *The thirteene bookes of Æneidos*. London 1584]

—[*Works*] *Eclogues, Georgics, Aeneid*. Trans H.R. Fairclough. Loeb Classical Library. 2 vols. 1918; rev ed, London and Cambridge, Mass 1934
Wallace, Malcolm W. *The Life of Sir Philip Sidney*. 1915; rpt New York 1967
Warkentin, Germaine. 'Sidney's Certain Sonnets: Speculations on the Evolution of the Text.' *The Library* 6th ser 2 (1980) 430–44
Warton, Thomas. *History of English Poetry*. Ed W.C. Hazlitt. 4 vols. 1871; rpt Hildesheim 1968
Webster, John. '"The Methode of a Poete"; An Inquiry into Tudor Conceptions of Poetic Sequence.' *English Literary Renaissance* 11 (1981) 22–43
Wells, Stanley and Gary Taylor. *Three Studies in the Text of Henry V*. Oxford 1979
Whiting, Bartlett Jere. *Proverbs, Sentences, and Proverbial Phrases from English Writings Mainly before 1500*. Cambridge, Mass 1968
Williams, Franklin B., Jr. *Index of Dedications and Commendatory Verses in English Books before 1641*. London 1962
Williams, John Edward, ed. *English Renaissance Poetry: A Collection of Shorter Poems from Skelton to Jonson*. Garden City, NY 1963
Wilson, F.P. *The English Drama 1485–1585*. Ed G.K. Hunter. Oxford 1969
Winters, Yvor. 'The 16th Century Lyric in England' [1939].' Reprinted in *Elizabethan Poetry: Modern Essays in Criticism* ed Paul J. Alpers, pp 93–125. New York 1967.

Index of First Lines of Poems

An asterisk indicates a poem by Alexander Neville or Laurence Blundeston

General Index

The following combines an index of names in the introduction, commentary, and textual appendix with a checklist of words glossed in the commentary. The checklist does not necessarily give every occurrence of a word glossed.